The Choice and Other Stories

By

Augustine Imbuye Wasonga

Ariba Book Publishers

ISBN: 978-9966-1818-7-9

Ariba Book Publishers

P. O. Box 503-40600

Siaya –Kenya

Tel: +254 723 987926

Website: www.aribabp.com

Email; admin@aribabp.com

Printed by: Susmo Enterprises

P.O Box 345-00511

Nairobi-Kenya

First published-2014

DECLARATIONS

This book is a collection of stories written by the author from1991 to 2013, save for a few revisions.

As a reflection of life spanning over two decades, it is possible that one may find a character that resembles him or herself, or a scene that they would identify with. This book however has fictitious characters and scenes that reflect the author's imagination.

ACKNOWLEDGEMENT

I acknowledge the help in typing I got from my wife, Rosemary Moraa Angwenyi and my Colleague, Damaris Wanza Muasya. I also acknowledge my family that gave me the peace and tranquillity to write down these reflections.

DEDICATION

This book is dedicated to my late father and mother for they shaped to a large measure the way I look at life.

THE CHOICE

John Mark was a good family man. He had Married 10 years ago when his first born son, James threatened to be born out of Wedlock.

The wedding ceremony itself was not an embarrassment. His wife Loyce was not one of those creatures whose stomachs distended guiltily when carrying a child. When you saw it slightly rise, you knew that she was almost ready to be sentenced to a maternity ward. So all this was well concealed and as the pastor intoned his priestly abracadabra, every member of the congregation felt that this was a well matched and behaved couple. They even decried the fact that girls nowadays gave birth before marriage and few of them ever brought their choices to be blessed at the altar.

Good boy, this John Mark. He had been an altar boy and everyone agreed that he missed being a priest by inches. Still, he would make a good pillar. In fact one old man decided to broach it in their next meeting that he be elected one of their church elders.

For their honeymoon- which they had in fact taken an advance of- they went to Mombasa. The doctor had advised Loyce that she needed the weather in her final month. So they went and stayed there for a complete month. Then the child came and John Mark arranged for her to stay with some discrete friends at the coast, before she recovered enough to travel and go to college. She was going to finish her final year at the local university, majoring in economics. Not bad for a businessman, he decided.

When he came from honeymoon many people were expecting to see his bride. He didn't tell them she had given birth to a
strong sturdy boy called James, but claimed she was living with his relatives and would go to college from there. Not many questions were asked. For a whole year and seven months, John Mark's friends were not to see his wife but then he was also rarely at home. He was a successful businessman with a chain of stores at the age of 30 and therefore, he was justified to be away for long periods on business trips. By now, he was one of the twelve church elders and the pastor sanctioned the move hastily,

seeing a source of income for harvesting more souls to Christ. And John Mark gave generously. The man was so innovative, a genius at raising money. So the brother in Christ was well loved all round.

At one time, John Mark let it slip in church that a son had been born to them. They were enthusiastic to see the baby but then the mother was still at college. Well, blast the woman; they decided she should be staying with them more often. When she finally appeared on the scene the second time their baby was walking. People wondered, and in fact one man let it be known that the boy had grown too fast. But this was brushed aside in the general euphoria of having John Mark's wife to be one of them. And just imagine this time she was here to stay!

She would be working with an NGO as a project officer, quite a lucrative post. And what a loving couple they were! And their child James was growing up into a lovely boy! Soon, Loyce was consigned to the maternity again. She took exactly two days and gave birth to a baby girl and they promptly named her Mary Magdalene, in memory of that indefatigable woman, who, together with Jesus mother had held vigil next to the tomb. As a matter of fact, they were the first to be addressed by an angel after Jesus' death.

There was a third notable birth. It was notable because it came exactly a year after that of Mary Magdalene and this time God blessed them with twins, a boy and a girl. One, the boy, they named Josiah and the girl they called Esther. That done, they finished with multiplying and filling the earth.

In church, they were an exemplary couple, contributing promptly; they were members of almost all groups within the church. The base of John Mark was incomplete if the soprano of Loyce didn't ring out. Here was a well read and rich couple who integrated well with them. Their simplicity was quite infectious.

And they really loved one another. Always you would see them walking hand in hand in perfect bliss. It was as their youth was just blossoming.

Every wedding, the pastor made sure they were the Bible verse on which to base his sermon. They never raised a voice against one another, either in private or in public. Their love is what was said to be deep .And they raised their children well. They turned out to be well behaved and James was already playing the piano for the choir. Nothing disrupted their life.

One time, people began noticing that John Mark's business trips were becoming longer and longer. In fact, it was an issue which dominated one of their family discussions. Loyce felt that his continuous absences was dictated by excuses rather than reasons. And she was beginning to miss her man. But John Mark convinced her of the necessity of the trips.

Then there was a time he returned from a business trip. He was looking dishevelled and guilty. And around him hang an aroma of a feminine perfume she was sure he didn't use. She wondered the origin when rummaging through his briefcase when he was in the bath (again a strange occurrence: they normally bathed together). She came across some lipstick and some concealed condoms. She was sure they never used the condoms since they had agreed that she was to take the birth control measure. On further search, she found a room reservation ticket for some county hotel in the name of Mr and Mrs John Mark. Still it didn't make sense John Mark was a man of surprises and maybe he had something waiting for her.

When he came out of the bathroom, dressed and fresh, he was again the perfect family man. He inspected their children's homework and helped them out where necessary. Soon it was time for supper, which was taken in perfect family bliss and thereafter John Mark led them in prayers for the might. As they went to bed, they discussed a wide range of issues, but still, he didn't broach the idea of the hotel reservation.

The two weeks they had together passed on remarkably well. In fact, she almost forgot the evidence she had seen and dismissed her fearful thoughts as childish. She clung to John Mark more and more and her man responded splendidly. Then one day he told her that he'd be going for a weeklong tour of his projects. Her heart sank for a fleeting moment.

'Have you to stay away that long, my love?

'Dear, it is extremely necessary. Every now and then you have to inspect the books'.

'But- I am on leave, you could give me something to do'.

'Oh, I forgot about that'.

'So what am I to do?' She pressed

'In fact let me just inspect them this once, then I can bring you an update report. From then on you will save me the fatigue of running around. By the way, we are putting up a new petrol station'

'A petrol station! Why didn't I know we were expanding that much?'

'It is necessary; it is not good to keep money idly in the bank'.

'Yes. That's true'.

'So goodbye my dear'

'I am so glad I married you. Travel well darling'. With that, they kissed, perfect partners parting.

It was when the vehicle was out of sight that she realized she had not asked him about the hotel reservation. She rang his office to enquire from his secretary whether she had been instructed to cancel it. She said no. She asked her if she saw any booking receipt in his personal file in the office. After a long search during which Loyce thought the lady had rang off, she came back on the line.

'Yes Hello, I thought you hang up'

'I am afraid I can't see any receipt'

'Are you sure?'

'Quite'

'And where does he normally stay when on business trips? It must be reflecting on his expenses'

'I am sorry I don't Know'

'All right. Goodbye and thank you'

'Thank you Madame'

It was strange. She could not relate this business. She decided to ring the hotel.

'Hello?'

'Hello there can I help you?'

'This is Mrs John Mark. Are you expecting us?"

'Yes, your husband confirmed in the morning. He said food is to be sent up....... when are you arriving?
'I don't know, but should beabout 6 pm' she lied.
'Alright Madame first class service"
'I'll remember'
She sat numb. Then she rose and without telling anyone where she was going. She took their old Volkswagen and stepped on the accelerator. The Beatle rattled, heaved and sighed, but she was oblivious of her protests.
At 6.30pm, she had reached the hotel and was thankful enough at seeing their car already packed. She parked the Beatle next to it and hurriedly left it, hoping to rescue her husband from the mouth of what in her mind now was represented a beast.
In the same breadth, she was at the reception, looking for the key room.
'But he has already gone in" said the receptionist.
'I know but he'll be busy reading'
'We don't normally issue out both keys to a room"
'Know but remember you said first class service'
'Well, you can get it but I'll send someone to fetch it.......when? Shall I say in 15 minutes time?
'Yes. It will be all over by then.' she replied, picking the key and bouncing up the stairs.

On reaching door 213A, she paused to gain her breath .She didn't want to faint on getting in. She gave her last prayers to God to save her eyes from seeing an unspeakable abomination. Above all she asked for divine guidance in destroying the monster that now like a python must be wound around her husband, choking out his moral sensibilities. The thought was overwhelming. She felt her knees weaken and sat down, her heart palpitating dangerously, her breath coming in long fitful gasps. She felt the world dancing twist around her. She looked at the well-polished ceiling and the neon light that hang on it, producing a romantic effect, as if to mock her.

At that, she felt rejuvenated, stood up and as true as daylight inserted the key into the lock. The lock was well oiled and opened without complaint. She entered and could at first see nothing clearly. She saw the table and the

5

remains of coffee standing neglected, the cups like two sentinels oblivious of the battle raging at the behind the next door. She could see her husband, his back turned on her, lowering his trousers.

The bedside lamp was lit. It was red neon and she could not focus properly on what was there.
Then her eyes accustomed to the haze and she saw the monster lying on her back, thighs slightly parted as if in anticipation, looking longingly at him, lips parted and eyes closed in thrilling trepidation. Her breasts were lolling languidly on her soft chest, heaving by every purring breadth.

Like a whirlwind, she had knocked down her husband who gave a surprised yelp before she leapt at the wench, covering her with her body. The woman gave out a soft moan and a sigh of expectation, still unaware of the meaning of the weight on her. Then she was there looming large as death, tearing at her beautiful face and pounding her with every part of the body. Her body felt hot and she perspired fearing the tigress was mauling her. She tried and tried to kick for her life. Then she discovered it was a human being, a woman and almost immediately found breathing space and slipped from the bed. She was hyperventilating. As she half saw half felt the tigress coil for another attack, she turned on her and caught the hem of her skirt and started pulling her across the room.

The attacker lost balance and followed her as a faithful but tired dog. After going around the bed twice, she dashed the attacker against the bathroom door which burst open with the weight of the victim who got deposited on the toilet seat with her buttocks. She was prevented from falling sideways because the toilet was wedged in between two grudging walls. Her head rolled forward and the girl saw that this was her lover's wife.

In a flurry, she started putting on forgetting her pant, which one discovered John Mark had worn over and above his trousers and was now peeping from behind just where his coat tail ended. He was trying to push papers into his briefcase when his wife recovered from her shock and without notice, again leapt at her husband's lover. The two fought fiercely and everything in the room except for the bed was breaking up. The two cups of coffee were suddenly knocked off balance as the table was pulled to act as artillery in battle. They did a Russian jig, somersaulted on the air and then fell down with double tinkering racket that jangled the nerves of John Mark.

He knew that if he attempted to stop the battle, he'd be ground to pulp. His mind worked in a whirl. His frame was torn asunder by two opposing forces-intervention and hibernation-that made it be rooted unmoving the same spot. Then an idea let his mind.
He jumped on the window and sat on it. The room was on the 10th floor and the result would be instant death if he dropped down.

"Look" he shouted to the battling tigresses; I am going to jump down and die unless you stop the fight!'
The two paused for a moment unable to comprehend. Then in the lull, he made an ultimate confession and ultimatum.
'Oh my dears, Ilove you both and I don't want to lose any of you. If you continue to fight I'll drop down and die. Then you'll both lose me'

The result was electric. They lost their concern with one another and started pleading with their lover to come down. Each called him by his pet names.
Mama James said.

'Ah my man, Mon Cherie, why do you want to leave this way? Please remember our vows, o you good Christian soul, remember you'll not go to heaven if you murder yourself. Father of my children Mylove is greater than my shame.
At this he threatened further to drop and his girlfriend added her voice.
'Please, please, my love, my dear. You have given meaning to my life. Didn't I give birth to your child and vow to keep it out of public? Please, please, remember our vow to love and love and love. Where will I turn to if you die? Your name will be desecrated and you know how much we love each other and how I have protected your public image. Oh dear, all will be dashed like a guard against a stone!'

He began looking mollified after this and more entreaties he stepped down after making them agree to make peace and not to tell anyone. For the first time, the family of Mr and Mrs John Mark invited their former secretary Agnes, who he had sacked two years earlierfor pregnancy and disreputable conduct as their guest in the house. They arrived home at 11 pm in the night and found their children sleeping. When people saw Agnes leave their house the next morning, there was talk of reconciliation and the magnanimity of Mr and Mrs John Mark won rounds of applause. The pastor vowed to talk to the Bishop to ordain this good Christian soul as deacon or appoint him a canon of faith!

VISITATIONS

The man left his class at 11.10 am dog tired after trying to push through some knowledge into minds of his form 3 girls. He left them an assignment which he was sure they were unenthusiastic about as they had been about his strenuous calculations on the board. But what do you do? He sighed, suddenly thankful for the end of the lesson bell rescuing him from the bored stare of the students-girls, as the saying goes, are not supposed to be gifted in mathematics and sciences. Damn the theory, he thought, viciously kicking a piece of paper fallen on the ground and angrily commanding a girl pretending to be from the loo to pick it up.

Not a bad girl, he mused, leaving the staffroom. Should grow into a star..........but she has already started following me uncomfortably to give solutions to her mathematical problems. No, it's not mathematics, it is something...

Suddenly, the laughter from the staffroom burst into his consciousness. It must be time for tea. Teachers are often gloomy except when they can get an opportunity to eat without paying. The inflation crunch... I am sure some are taking their breakfast here .He greeted colleagues all around chatting here and there a moment too long with his close comrades and contributing to the overall effect of a market place din.

Three or so students were standing meekly in front of their teachers, quarrelling with them or giving them orders about this and that as concerns class work. One teacher spoke to a student in vernacular and expected herto answer in English or Kiswahili, the latter which he understood little.Another teacher was recalling loudly to colleagues how he used to cross valleys and brave even the heaviest rains in the darkest nights to go to village parties every time secondary school students sponsored a jig. He remembered a girl-here it was agreed by consent that no student should be in the staffroom and even the ones bringing exercise books for marking were unceremoniously turned back-,a daughter of a leading light in their locations and a real beauty whom he used to take out through the fence as their father's steel gate stood locked by a vicious looking padlock. One day, while fleeing the chief's *askaris* from an illegal village disco, she fell

9

bottom flat on a pool of mud and when they went to his cubicle, she sat on his bed on which he had spread white sheets belonging to his sister for the occasion...

The school secretary, Miss Jaldesa (no one understood why she was called Miss Jaldesa; she was married with five children and the husband worked with the Ministry of Public works- *Apida*- and came every month end with the hope of planting another seed) came in and tapped him on the shoulder. Mwalimu, there is a visitor for you by the gate. He lingered for a minute to hear the end of the story but half of the staff was still guffawing with laughter and the rest wiping tears off their eyes. He decided to go to the gate, wondering who the visitor might be. He had just seen his parents during the weekend and a brother was staying with him. Most of his friends would have just burst into the staffroom to look for him anyway.

By the time the thought dried up, he had reached the school gate. He gave a passing glance to a strange girl of about 14 who stood meekly by the gate and a workman trimming the fence. He went to the gatepost but the gateman was not in his cubicle. He checked the visitors list but didn't see any name he recognized. Just as he was about to go past the gate to his house in the local market centre in the hope that the visitor had changed his or her mind and went to his house instead. The day watchman hailed him from behind. "Mwalimu! That girl is your visitor."
"Oh"

He stopped on his tracks. His mind was blank. He could not register seeing this girl anywhere in the universe, not even he mused, in his fertile dreams.
"What is your name?"
"Mimi niAneshe" ("Am Aneshe")
'*UnatokawapiAneshe?*' ("Where do you come from?")
'*NimetokahukoBGM*'("Am from BGM")
'*BGM niupandegani?* '('Where is BGM?')
Bungoma nihukomasharikimwakenya'(Bungoma is in Western Kenya)
'Oh' He dried up again trying to dig up any connection: he utterly failed.
'*Na unatabugani?* '('And what's your problem?')

'Antiindioalinisendnikuleteebaruahii.' ('My aunt sent me to bring this letter to you')

At this point, she fished out a letter from a polythene bag she had been carrying. He swiftly glimpsed inside and saw what looked like two knitting pins, a ball of thread and a beginning of a cardigan. Funny he mused as he read his name boldly spelt out at the back of the envelope, unable to recognize even the hand writing. This is not even from a girlfriend, present or former he thought, decisively. He wished to question the girl further but realized the gateman and the grounds-man trimming the fence were within earshot, pretending not to pay attention. Any embarrassing moments with his visitor might spread within minutes as subject of gossip. So he shepherded the little girl out of the school gate towards his house. As they walked, he tried to steal sidelong glances at the innocent girl meekly walking by his side in order to establish any connection. He utterly failed.
He began whistling a popular tune to drive off worries crossing his mind, convincing himself that the issue will be settled when he opens the letter in his house.

Presently they reached his house and he took the key from his neighbour's house, after realizing his house was locked despite the reggae beat booming from his 'system', a Lanico Trident hifi with woofers and subwoofers that he bought on loan from African Retail Traders (ART) on a 36 months' pay-as you –use scheme and was attracting pleasant female prospects every day.

He opened the door, welcomed the young girl to seat and discreetly sat a bit far, and pretending coolness, opened the letter. It run thus.

Judy Masinde
P.O Box Private Bag
BGM.
Dearest and Sweet Darling,

11

I am happy beyond expression to write to you after a long spell of silence.

Actually, I have been thinking of you day and night, hoping for the day that I'll announce to you the happy news- a dear son has been born to you...

Here, he nearly crumbled the letter and half –stood from his seat before he realized he had a guest in the house. He looked up guiltily at the young girl who by now was knitting unconcernedly, waiting until she will be addressed. Then he thought of a beautiful idea. Send her to the kitchen. Then he told her to be free to go and make some tea in the kitchen. The little girl dutifully did as she was bid.
Then he continued reading...

In fact my precious love, your son is an exact replica of you and through him, your image, which was fleeting during the painful but proud moments when I carried him in my womb, is now more firmly etched in my mind.

I do not know whether you will want to remain with him when I go back to finish my third year at college, we will discuss that when I come with him.But for now, give my sister money for the following .Alternatively you could buy them yourself, so that their prices might not shock you when you remain with Picasso-that's the name I've given him after a great painter-remember I am a fine arts student.
10 Napkins
250 grams Vaseline Baby Jelly
Cussons Baby Powder

Cussons Baby Soap
1Kg Nun Baby food
1kg Cerelac Baby Food
4 Baby Shawls
1 Trough for bathing Baby
Assorted Baby clothes, Socks and Shoes.
All these items, my sweet dear, I have estimated to come to 3,500 KShs. I also want you to provide 1,000 KShs. for the baby's milk monthly and 500 for the maid every month.
Please give Aneshe the items listed above for the baby and also tell her the date you expect me to bring for you your baby. Remember to refund her transport coming- I borrowed from our neighbour and her transport back to Bungoma. In all, 500.
Goodbye
Loving,
Judy (Mama Pics).

For a long time he sat with head blank. Halfway through the list, his mind had already travelled to a long time ago in his past several hundred miles from his house. He could not comprehend the whole thing and was tempted to dismiss it as a bad joke. But no. A joke could not be extended this far.

He remembered their first meeting lazily, especially as it had been when he had taken a bottle more than normal. It was a party organised for students from his district. He had drank and danced till about one O'clock when he had noticed the girl dancing by herself and realized that he too had no girl.

He had swaggered to her, wobbling and careening over to her, embraced her and asked her to the dance floor. Surprisingly, she had accepted. After that they got inseparable and as the swahili's would say, 'kamapetenachanda'. So he did not remember anything special except waking up in a strange bed the next morning. On looking around, an imitation of the statue of Mary had stared at him coldly and various art paintings decorated the room to taste. He had looked around cautiously and had seen the lady in question sitting next to a mirror, methodically doing her hair. He had done something with his throat to alert the lady who looked at him with a broad smile that rankled his bowels. He looked for his trouser but before he could see them, the Lady had miraculously produced them and jokingly flung the beddings from him before planting a kiss on his cheek.

That is when he realized he was totally naked. He assumed that things had happened.
He could not find his underpants. The girl told him she had washed them for him and would he mind getting them later from her room or would she bring them over? He must have mumbled his address to the lady to escape and lied about an overdue term paper on Ethics before fleeing the room. As he walked, he could almost hear his manhood jingling with guilt in his buggy trousers. That was the first big surprise.
"Tea is ready"
He nearly jumped out of his chair as he was brought back to harsh reality and the present.
"Yes, yes, yes. Set the table"
He said and went back to his reverie, promising to be half awake to his surroundings.

The second major surprise was another day when they were planning to go to a birthday party with a friend. He was just tying his tie when they heard a knock on the door. His friend opened, impatient at whoever it was that would delay their departure and make it one beer less. Here he stirred the tea and started sipping.

As he turned to go out, he confronted a smiling girl and he broke into a broad smile thinking that an infectious good humour will make her say her business quickly. Then she said I see you are planning to go out. But I have something pressing to give you. She had a small parcel wrapped and written –'With love from Judy'. His friend had noticed a certain unease and guilt that enveloped his face and told him they'd meet at the party.

14

When he unwrapped the gift, he found it was his under pant and despite his reservations, they broke into laughter. He then rubbed all doubts as to his visitors identity and without knowing how, he found himself in her arms.

He woke up with a start when it was dark and switched on his room light. It was one o'clock. Something stirred next to him and he realized it was the girl. He cursed her softly under his breath and burnt with rage wishing to strangle her. Well, as clear as daylight, 'things had happened' again. 'Shit!!!'
'Mwalimu Unamwanga Chai kwakiti!' Teacher you're splashing tea on to the chair!, Well'... He woke up to his surroundings.

To hell with that girl and now this.......he crumpled the letter and prepared to throw it out the window then he changed his mind and put it in his pocket. The girl had gone to get something to mop up the tea.

When the girl came back, he had changed his face and smilingly asked.
'When are you expected home?'
'Today evening' she replied
'Okay, wait for me a bit.'
'How long?'
'I will be back lunch time. You can prepare some lunch.
'What am I to cook?'
'You will find some eggs on the shelves and some unga too'.

He rushed out of the room, his mind in a whirl. He had to do something about this but he had to think first. One thing was clear: it was time he took the initiative.

First, he went to the school. The Staffroom was now quiet. But he found a colleague he was looking for, a History teacher who complained to him that a student had just written in a test that it was William Wilberforce who found the source of the Nile.

He led him out of the staffroom and enquired of him if he might lend him 1500/-.

15

The teacher agreed without asking any questions and shortly he was on his way to his house again. When he reached his house there was tantalizing smell lazily wafting from his kitchen.

He remembered the cassette player which stopped sometimes back and turned on the Radio. It was after news and a session of music had set in a relevant number came over the waves: 'Shida'. It played as the table was set.

At lunch, they had small talk with the girl. He was trying to pry innocuously. He learnt she had just started form one. He went and plugged in Bob Marley's 'Uprising' and the number 'No Woman no Cry' came on play. Then he remembered he had a double lesson in the afternoon session. That's why I hate Tuesdays, he reckoned. I will have to teach Physics to a sleeping class and I'll be half asleep myself.

He gave the girl the One Thousand five hundred shillings to take to her sister, and sent her off, hoping to puzzle out his misfortune before the class. He kept wondering how she knew he had come to teach in this school after college. Strange are ways of women, he thought, going to pick a chalk from the staffroom and planning what to teach as the bell for the lesson rang.

By the time he moved from the staffroom to the class, the lesson plan was already sketched in his mind. He decided to teach Archimedes Principal, since it was an area he was well rehearsed in and he could not remember teaching it to the class. He took the duster and rubbed the board himself-something he rarely did-slowly as if savouring the joy of it all. Then he turned to the class and told them: 'Good morning Class'
'Oh Good Afternoon Mwalimu'
And the students burst into laughter. He was scandalized so much but since he did not want to pour his rage on them, he kept completely quiet, which made the laughter die just as abruptly as it had started.

He lost his wits as he taught listlessly unaware that he was slipping into his private thoughts). The students realised something was amiss when for a whole two minutes he stood, blankly looking at them, his eyes fixed at something just over their heads. One not very mischievous student felt she had the dubious duty of asking him what the problem was.

He realized he was being asked if he was feeling normal and still thinking he was teaching, he answered no. When he 'came to his senses' he realized his mistake, mumbled an excuse about some severe headache and 20 minutes into the lesson he walked out, with students giving audible sighs of relief at the windfall. They were particularly thankful that for the first time since he had started teaching them, he had forgotten to give them an assignment. Of course he was working too hard, they agreed, wishing he could teach them religious education instead.

He walked to the staffroom, his mind in a whirl. He found the staffroom noisy again. Some teachers had finished their days work but instead of knocking off, they decided to make the staffroom lively. Somebody asked him why he didn't finish teaching his lesson. But before he could reply, the headmistress passed through the staffroom to her office, and every teacher hurriedly pulled something out and got busy. He concentrated on studying the time table as if it was a strange object fallen from the outer space. A few teachers took their chances and slunk away, hoping to return at 4 O'clock when they could not be blamed for being lazy. He accompanied two teachers to a staff mate's house to listen to some music and talk in a more liberal atmosphere.

In this liberal atmosphere he fell asleep on the chair and on waking up found his staff mates gone leaving him a note on where he could look them up.
'Just as well' he mused, suddenly thankful. He went-out to his house where he found his brother had returned and reggae calypso was again blaring from the lungs of the speakers. He confirmed with him if there was food for supper and on getting an affirmative answer, he went to his bedroom, asking his brother not to tell any visitor he was around.
Well, time he thought. Here was his life, like an egg balanced on a string. And as time as the position of your nose, any slight motion would smash it to smithereens. He was not prepared for that, but the chain of action had been triggered.

17

First, who told that girl where I was posted? None of my friends knew I had an embarrassing liaison with the girl. They didn't know her and he was sure she didn't know his friends. He had introduced her to none, knowing that whatever happened between the two of them was not anything to write home about. That left his friends clean and brought a new, frightening if dawning possibility. The lady might have an influential mole at TSC who rummaged through almost 10,000 files of new postings to find out where he was posted; or she got her information from the Dean of Education. In both cases, this girl had shown a determination to trap him quite unprecedented. In a nutshell, this would be a hard nut to crack.

Secondly, why does this lady assume so much that I will just accept her schemes? Well, in the first case, it was me who approached her. But any girl in her senses would know that I didn't love her, much less desire her to such absurd proportions. Of course that time she came to my room...but why did she want it so much? After all I only did it as a way of disposing her quickly and making sure she didn't tag at my collar for the rest of the night. And I thought there was a tacit agreement that there was, and will be nothing further between us. Now she was breaking the agreement with impunity. Her arrogance might mean she is more than prepared to trap me at all costs....He felt a coldness pass sideways across his stomach, criss-crossing with a warmth from his rib cage, down his navel and ending in waves at his man pike completing a cross.

The criminal, he cursed softly, believing that had it refused to function, at least for that night in his room when he was sure things happened, he would not be in this mess........ .

Thirdly, there was this possibility of marriage. It was remote, yes, but one had to be psychologically prepared for. Supposing the lady decided to take him to court, especially now that she'd shown she'll stop at nothing-what course of defence will be open to him? He could deny and that will trigger off investigations that might well prove costly for him. But if he accepted he was responsible and said he'd marry the girl? The judge would ask them to settle it out of court. Then he could marry her and neglect them-something hard to prove in court. During such a lull, he will be able to prepare himself by learning just what monster he was dealing with. Well, why not marry her? I'll broach the idea to my parents this Saturday.

This settled, he set himself for the long wait until she would come one day, carrying a puny little thing she call Picasso that's supposed to be his child. The day proved to be elusive as a will o' the wisps but it finally came. During the wait, sometimes he would wake up at 1 am and stare at the ceiling in darkness for the rest of the night. He would toss and toss and toss in his sleep and sometimes profusely feverish and nervous.

But the day as sure as a call of nature, finally arrived. Its arrival marked a fourth major surprise this lady had sprung to him. There had been no warning that afternoon that he had a visitor. In fact, at 4pm, he had gone for games, since he was coaching the school hockey team and they were due to have a tournament during the weekend. They played up to 6 pm and as he went home, he marvelled at the improvement of the team. He already could see a good goalkeeper and a good back combination that would render their goalmouth impenetrable.

The only problem was in the striking force, but that could be adjusted with time and relying on chance, they could prove a major upset to the established 'hockey authorities'. On reaching his house, he was surprised to find the door open, an unusual thing since his brother was not due back for another two days. Even the child crying somewhere in his bedroom did not register to him. His mouth wet with saliva as he smelt an aromatic scent that like a billowing smoke seemed to fill the house and too hung pregnable on the air in the house. He decided whoever had raided his kitchen was bent on surprising him.

He proceeded to the bedroom where he got his first shock. There on his bed, a baby lay wrapped in a soft shawl. He removed his sports shoes and looked for his sandals. That was when he got another shock. Where he normally put his sandals, they were not to be seen. But their place was taken by some red female shoes which rang a bell. He decided he had seen this make of shoes somewhere. He then determined to confront this person, whoever it was, raiding his privacy. His neighbour's wife was not this indecent. But that is where he normally kept his house key. He padded into the sitting room and as he crossed to the kitchen, he saw someone emerge from the bathroom carrying her clothes to cover her breasts and womanhood. She was only wearing a panty and was smiling broadly at him as if to announce his impending sojourn to heaven.

He could not comprehend the joke. He slightly averted his eyes so as to see what would not like somebody to see in public or in private unless under oath and almost at the same time, the door opened and his local girlfriend came in and stopped, rooted at the door. It was the all but naked ambush lady who saved the situation by welcoming her to sit and excusing herself so that she could go and make herself more decent. He took the opportunity and dashed into the bathroom, feeling the eyes of his girlfriend boring at and singeing his back. He closed the door and turned on the shower as he took off his clothes.

He slowly applied soap to his head and face and rinsed off, wondering who the visitor was and the explanation he'll have to make to Marie. Just as he was applying soap to his body taking his time, the bathroom was pounded by force that left its rotting hinges rattling in palpitating after waves of an explosion. Then an injunction was issued.

Don't hide in the bathroom come out and tell me who this dog is and what you were doing with her! That left him cold. Marie had to understand his situation, he didn't even know the strange lady and here she was making riot with him, not caring about the scandal she'd bring. He decided it was time to dump her and he made an injunction in his mind expelling both Marie and the strange lady, kit and caboodle, their kith and kin, connections, friends of agents from ever stepping again in his house. Just then, the strange lady came out of the bedroom and asked what the visitor was doing around. Marie must have jumped on her throat because he heard a cry like a stifled laughter and before you could say Prudence Bushnell, he was bathed and out to avert possible murder tying only a towel around his waist.

Marie saw this and turned her wrath on him, leaving the ambushing visitor sitting on her backside gasping for breath. Before he could take his eyes from the wreckage to Marie, she had wiped off the towel from him in a whirl like a ballet dancer, leaving him naked and ashamed. She used this as a whip on his bare back and turned to the ambushing visitor who was by now standing. Just then, neighbours started pounding the door which must have been locked and as the ambushing visitor remembered to open it for escape, he remembered his nakedness just in time and dashed into the bedroom.

"Wuii, she's killing us!"

'What is it?' Shouted a neighbour as the door finally opened. 'I will not tolerate this harlot coming into my house'

'But what is it?' put in another.

'It is this lady who has burst into our house and started beating us' cried the ambushing visitor, shaking like a leaf.

'Are you his wife?' asked a mischievous female teacher who also lived next door. Both Marie and the ambushing lady answered simultaneously yes' yes' and as they were about to fly for each other necks again, the silence that momentarily hung like the moment following the flash of lightening before the thunder was rent by piercing cries of the baby who had been forgotten, and no one had counted on.

Immediately, the man walked out of the bedroom, dressed in a stonewash and T-shirt to match and calmly gave the baby to the mother before asking both the lady and Marie to come in. He was so calm that quiet reigned like a vicious king and one by one, the onlookers started drifting away. Both ladies also sat meekly, facing one another ashamedly, hanging their heads as children do when found in mischief.

'Now' he begun, and paused just enough to shift some phlegm of anger blocking his throat: 'You both see the shame and disrepute in which you have dragged my name.' Here, he paused again for dramatic effect. He continued:

'Perhaps you don't know one another. I'll introduce you. Marie here has been my girlfriend for some time. But that will not be necessary from today we will sever all the links between us henceforth and any other subsequent meeting between us should be like that between distant friends.' He paused again and saw the face of Judy gleaming with pride of 'I knew I will win' attitude.

'Judy Masinde here '-he said shifting his gaze to rest squarely on the woman who was by now breastfeeding the baby-'was an acquaintance at college. To be exact, this is our third meeting. But I am told that the child she is carrying is my baby.' Marie almost flew up in rage.

'Be that as it may be, both of you will be undesirable visitors in this house as from this day .I will allow both of you to stay the night but you must leave early tomorrow for your homes. And I repeat again- and he paused – and again: whoever shall bring riot in this house will meet my fearful wrath today."

He concluded his little speech. None of them could talk. He then rose and said as he went out. 'I will be back for supper at 9.00pm.'

He went to the house of the Madame teacher and after they had some coffee they stayed, talking and talking until it was time to watch a TV Programme 'The Rich Also Cry,' to which he was an indefatigable customer.

They didn't mention the little scene in his house at all and when the programme ended, he rose and bid her bye, with an understanding not to breath the storm to anyone, especially among the staff.

He entered his house and found the two women talking and laughing and the table set for supper. He saw it was chicken and did not ask how it was procured. He assumed it had to do with the smell that had hit him as he had first entered the house from school. He looked at the baby who was now sleeping, innocently unaware of what might have gone on. He had no feeling towards him-in fact none are for the mother of Marie. He had undergone a moral crisis that evening and was now placid.

After supper, he talked with Judy and she agreed to take a monthly allowance of 600/- for the baby. There and then, he gave her 1,000/- and then settled their sleeping arrangements. He would forgo his bed for them.

The next Morning as he was going to school, both Marie and Judy were off, perfect friends. He resolved not to leave his key again at the neighbour's house and to add an additional lock. He was not sure it was all over for he planned to pay only for one month and stop that as well...

LETTER TO A FRIEND

My dear Irene, It is such a long time since I heard from you and you – I am sure – from me. You are perhaps wondering what went wrong. Perhaps you are belabouring under the mistaken notion that the friendship between us was just superficial. Granted we grew up together and have related only as a brother and a sister would – not that it would have been wrong had we decided to throw romance into the works, you know. This kind of relationship should make me more attached to you…

Being a romantic man in my youth, (but I bore you with all these . You know me too well. Are you not the one who used to call for me those girls? Surely you do remember you are the one who helped me win over my first ever girlfriend?) , I cannot tell you with a straight face that I have reformed my errant ways. But I am jumping the story I wanted to tell you…

You remember the time I was at college and you came to visit me? You must have noticed Tom? Tom was my best friend in college if your memory fails you. But you will remember him since he is the chap we did our attachment with at Isaho.

It happened this way. When we graduated, we decided to request for posting together. The government in its wisdom and to our chagrin and acute dismemberment decided to post us to one of those new districts in what is designated as arid and semi-Arid areas or ASAL'S as we normally refer to them in our dispatches. You know that there is very little agriculture you can practice in such areas, considering also that the area is peopled by nomads who have been in that business of spurious life for centuries.

So here I was except for Tom, trapped for six.

In such a set-up, we decided that one of us would remain at the headquarters to man the makeshift Manyatta which acted as our district Agricultural and Veterinary office. You may laugh but it won't do you good. The district commissioner stays in a worse house and uses his dilapidated land-river as an office. But we don't mind it. Imagine there is a phone, telex and fax machine! And we even managed to wriggle a computer out of Nordic Aid Agency!

Anyway we decided that one of us was to wait for any administrative duties at the office while the other followed these nomads whom the Berlin conference was daft enough to lock us within the same borders with. We were not happy at being parted but we knew that when the push came to a shove, or rather when duty beckoned, one had to roll up one's sleeves and play ball. The next decision we had to make was on who would follow the seasonal migration and who would sweat it out in the makeshift 'District Headquarters'.

We decided to flip a coin. You can imagine why I took the interest in personally flipping it. First to stay in the office would mean constant cash-flow. Those who would come for vet services would be compelled to pay. Vouchers may be forged and tenders which would make one an instant millionaire if handled in the right way.... Don't forget a lot of government materials for building and construction of various structures. I am sure, Irene, that you would have chosen this option being a normal Kenyan.

But the alternative- your guess is right-was more to my liking. You know that amassing wealth has never been my idea of an interesting life. It would be boring. You'd only become greedy, greedier. Well, I had espied the beautiful nomadic girls and knew which side of my bread was buttered. I simply followed my instincts, sharpened by their scant dressing that by attempting to hide a precious little ended up baring all. Irene, these people are bizarre. Imagine they don't have blouses: And the skirts are just ribbons of cloth held together at the waist by a piece of string. It was too irresistible that I decided I was putting myself in a fatal position. I felt I was crossing the Rubicon!

So I waited when Tom was not concentrating and flipped the coin. My side came up like a fish that bobs up belly wise and unable to move is swept and slapped about by the waves. I could see tom smuggling preparing himself for his repose at the station and secretly saying-'serves you right'.

But I was also laughing at his foolishness and inability to discover the charms of nature and proceeding to feed on natures lap.

Off the trail started, single file, led but the numerous herds raising a stink of dust as they pioneered the routs. I had never seen anything like it. A human multitude led by herds of cattle, goats, donkeys and camels. They even presided over the pauses in the journey and the nomads did not complain. They even knew the water points. It was a route they had travelled for centuries. It was like a cavalry led by battering rams. I believe that if we met a creature in that wasteland, fright must have reigned so as to make the hapless creature faint. A marching army, marching into the unknown that is however known, marching on a mission to conquer nature that had enslaved them.

Of course Irene, you must have gotten the picture of what I was doing. You are right. I was watching the rise and fall of maidens' backsides, and many a maiden there was. I was quite incapable of deciding where to fix my gaze until it tripped on an ancient gnarled root of a tree which was in the process of weathering and piled on the hot sand. From then on, I decided that instead of rolling my neck in a 180 degree arc, I was better off fixing it for a lengthy interval, say, five minutes, on one before moving to the other. You can imagine the riot it caused in my groin. But you are not a man, moreover you have always given me the picture of being chaste, so you may not understand it all.

You are thinking, aren't you? That when night fell, I would mount one maiden then jump from her to the next. I must confess that I have no handicap in that direction. But these people are vastly different. Their culture is eons apart from ours. I don't intend to impute that they don't do it. Else how do they beget these maidens?

You must be wondering already what agriculture I was practicing all the while. I had titled my journey 'A survey of Agricultural possibility in the Isaho District of ASALS' – quite a pompous title. I had set off with the vague notion of convincing these people to be planting certain grains near water-points such that when it comes to the next migration season, they would be well provided for. I would say I succeeded to a measure, since these people amused themselves by doing my bidding especially in the evenings when they were resting at makeshift manyattas with no particular thing to do. They treated me as a child that needs to be indulged when adults were not busy.

They had, however noticed my interest in their maidens. Not going to school is never a handicap in such matters. These people are so wise and observant that they measure you up and put a price tag on you that should William Wilberforce have not abolished slave trade, they would have made fortunes. Instead of writing this letter to you I could be in the Mayflower or any ship with such a fancy name to America. My price, they deduced, was simple: I could go to any length to sleep with a woman. They had seen my darting ogling glances and knew exactly how to nurse the gravy train.

A sort of a religious leader came over to my tent on the seventh or so night of our wandering (you tend to lose track of time in such a primal atmosphere). He, moved with a deliberation that men of authority often affect, and spoke with what he believed to be a reverent voice. He told me what a fine young man I was, and that I was so handsome that he was seeing a competition among the women in the offing as to who would sleep with me. My spirit which had begun to flag took the whole force of the wind and stood erect, matched only by my bloated ego.

'But', he continued, we are a clan that are very religious, and only those who join the Islamic faith can relate with our women. But as it is young man, if in your heathen state you should be found in sinful relation with our women, then the code is clear; we will cut-off the offending part of your body'.
You can imagine how my organ shrank considerably before it cried out with some alarm:
'But that is beastly!'
'Then our women are also beastly'. He said and rose to leave the tent. He parted the flap that acted as its door and his figure disappeared. But a moment later he stuck his head back in, his toothless grim clearly illuminated by the setting sun and said:

'Tell me when you will start taking instructions to convert you to our faith'.

There I sat, Numb and dumb with trepidation and want. I was about to be trapped into a situation over which I had no control, but I was also hungry after the flesh of these forbidden maidens. I debated within myself and realized that I could not go back to the tent where Tom, I was by now convinced was thoroughly enjoying himself. I asked myself why I had not just flipped the coin the right way. Maybe I would have stayed at the 'district headquarters' and Tom would not be looking as dismal as I was.

You are well aware that my tie with the church has never been that strong. I was baptized, yes and confirmed. But apart from that I had always treated sermons as some kind of mumbo-jumbo, the trickery of the church to get the better of us. I have read the Bible well – from Genesis to Revelation. But there has never been a strong beginning to my faith, nor a prediction of a deem future to it. Of course I know the Sunday school injunctions that wisdom begin with the knowledge of God, and so on, as well as Jesus 'I am the truth, the way and the life'. I thought about all these as I sat in my tent and wondered what my next action would be.

'Farmer', a small feminine voice called from without. I nearly jumped up. The good people had given me a name and were not interested in knowing my real name. I guessed it was Aisha, The third daughter of Uthman, who was an influential and rich personage among the nomads, if wealth can ever be measured in terms of cattle, goats, camels and donkeys.
'Come in' I said, rising to welcome her. I had expressed my desire strongly to Aisha one such evening

When she had come to serve my supper three days earlier. Her family, the wealthiest, had been given the responsibility of my welfare. Uthman had eight daughters and countless sons (I was not keen). His two eldest daughters had already married and there was nothing to show for it although Uthman's herds had increased a hundredfold. The married daughters looked young and agile, full of spirit and quite untethered by their bonds of marriage, if you considered that the husband to the eldest had gone to Nairobi and would take as long as he likes, and the husband to the second was perpetually travelling ahead as some kind of scout to warn other nomads to move on and leave us space.

She parted the flap of the tent and entered slowly, a tall graceful girl who had to bend to get in, her breasts defying the rules or gravity. They were erect, challenging. You had to be a stone not to respond in kind and I responded as I had done before. But today I could not show it outwardly considering the warning of the 'Imam' that I would be 'Damned' if I offended the teachings of prophet Mohamed. Aisha seemed fairly disappointed and she asked me if I was sick.

'No' I said and felt sorry for being dour and taciturn. Aisha had learnt in the city and knew how to teach the nomadic children. She would teach them in the late afternoons as I taught the adults. We both provided distractions of some sort.
'Do you know how I can obtain the holy book?'
'Which Holy Book?' Aisha wanted to confirm.
'The Koran', I replied.
'Do you know how to read Arabic?'
'NO'
'Then I will get you one written in English. But why are you interested in the Koran?
'Well, I am…' I stammered and lapsed.
'Umph! You cannot cheat a small child. It must be Mahmoud was talking to you!'
By now I was well into my food and my spirits which had taken a nosedive began to soar again like a windsock. I decided to test the waters a bit.
'Would you be my lover if I converted to Islam?
'The heathen wants to go to heaven?' Aisha replied petulantly. 'How nice' she concluded.

It was all so frustrating. I had by now realized that these people are not keen on giving direct answers.
But Irene, you must have already guessed how I had rationalized myself into such a fix. My reasoning was; If God was God and God was supreme,

29

then it followed that it was only one God be one a Christian, a Muslim, a Hindu or any such religious mutation. So I decided that the greatest sin would be to betray God and I was not going to betray him, by changing from one religion to another. In any case he might be happy if he had been earlier bored by my Christian worship. I therefore felt that betraying a religion was no sin at all and I knew that I was going to become a Muslim even if it was to catch on the action I had been missing. I have been in this reverie when Aisha stood up from the floor, her sash revealing the intricacies of her thighs briefly before she came over to me. I stood up as if on impulse and she fell on my arms.

I was numb. I held her in that fashion for some time before realizing that there was a lot I could do. I kissed her for a long time, her mid-day breasts pressed against my chest till I felt my chest hollow and I believed they had pierced a hole through. Then she pulled away and told me: 'Too bad you are a heathen. I'd do anything for you if you were a follower of the prophet. I'll get for you the Koran.' She left me standing there, my mouth open from the lingering effect of the kiss as much as from wonder, and left a scent of femaleness that quite befuddled my thinking. 'Aisha' 'Aisha' 'Aisha....' I whispered severally, my heart smitten.

I roused myself from this reverie and decided to put an entry in my journal which indicated my conversion to Islam. I ended it with the words: 'Alahu Akbar!' which I thought meant 'God be praised!' The only doubt as to my full conversion which still lingered in my mind was the fact that I had not yet flayed a heathen in the name of the prophet. And it seemed as if I wouldnot have to wait long.

As I was preparing for bed, my name was again hailed in that soft caressing voice and I bid Aisha to come in. Mahmoud's warning had been enough and even though I was tempted, I could not play tango with Aisha. I opened for her, innocent as a lamb and chaste like a flower that blossoms in the morning and took the preferred Koran reverently. Aisha looked at me strangely, her eyes saying: 'If only you were a follower of the prophet...' The anything in the promise grew to be such a living thing that I was not left into any doubt of what it entailed.

The next day was spent under the tutelage of Mahmoud. He felt duty bound to guide me into the true faith as he put it. Over-night, people's reactions towards me had changed. They were freer to speak with me and there were no whispers when I approached. Maidens were never sternly warned if they gave me 'undue' attention.

As to my name, I decided to choose one that may sound pompous and impressive enough to get attention. I settled on Ismail Dan Fodio bin Batuta. My celebrity status as a heathen among the prophet's followers was stripped and replaced by one of a recent convert.

I hope, Irene that did not pick this letter when about to go bed, because there's still a lot more to relate. What made me love the faith more was the possibility of marrying four wives. Aisha had already told me that she would do anything for me. Khalida had not been looking at me badly either and Zainabu… Salima was also lurking in the background and I was not averse to giving her complementary glances. So I had my four wives planned out in advance and I knew what I would do with each….

Aisha never came back to my room during the next five days and on the sixth, I decided to marry her and get it over with. When I told Mahmoud Uthman of my predicament, he led me to Uthman, Aisha's father. He explained – they like talking in parables with a pinch of proverbs – that it was time Aisha got someone to look after her. Uthman looked at me sagely and nodded gravely, upon which he named his price. 'Fifty goats, five camels and twenty cattle. I was about to start whistling but the gesture gurgled in my throat. I swiftly calculated and saw that the bride price demanded was an equivalent of my six months wages which I had not started getting. I also thought that we would sojourn in the endlessness dessert for about the same duration so I did not let that thought constrain me.

By this time I was almost mad at my inability to get a woman to sleep with and was willing to go to any length in this pursuit. I had embarked on this journey by design and became a Muslim by calculation. I was now going

31

to get married by the same principle which in reality is lack of principles. But the thought of Aisha's 'I will do for you anything' was enough to fire me up like a brick.

'You have no herds with you here, 'Uthman said 'when do you give the bride price?'.
'As soon as we get back to the district headquarters, I said glibly knowing that the five remaining months would extricate me from whatever commitment I made.

Then Aisha was called and when she came she knelt in front of us. You know, Irene, what surprises me in this people is the respect they show to their men folk. They curtsey, they kneel, and they don't look their men in the eyes.... It is something one cannot get used to, something that adds a unique allures to their charms. As I looked at Aisha now, I was overwhelmed with want and an ambivalent feeling I couldn't put a finger on.

Finally the wedding was over and we were pronounced husband and wife before Allah.
Mahmoud congratulated me and I was informed by Uthman that there wouldbe a party at his tent that night when I would be given the bride officially. My heart began to thump erratically and soar at the same time I decided to suspend my 'classes' this evening. I licked my lips and knew that by evening I would be home and dry.

The matrimonial party came and went. I had not, likely a newlywed been just looking at my wife. She was captured, a bird in hand. I know that the British say in their folly that this is worth two in the bush. But I could not keep my eyes from moving.

They roved looking at the maidens performing their dances. During the dancing, I was careful to brush their backsides slightly while pretending to concentrate in my bride. What made me so charged up was the gyrations of their hips and the suppleness of their waists as they responded to the music. Their dancing is not like ours where women shake their shoulders and ululate. It does not involve the elaborate footwork you are used to, unless that footwork helps to move their hips and wriggle their waist. I tell you Irene, these people are full of allure.

Well, it was time and people departed. I wished them a good riddance and started towards my tent, my bride safely tucked under my arms. I was about to start a contented whistle when I noticed to my dismay and utter consternation that a group of old women and women had, notable among them Aisha's mother hadsurrounded my tent. I asked Aisha what was the matter and she squeezed my arm and whispered that it was alright. But her words could not comfort me. The play I had directed was crumbling before my eyes. The actors were there but they were at the wrong parts of the set.

When we reached and came to a halt before them, (I could not use my body as a battering ram, to cut a swathe through them, especially as I needed every ounce of energy I could preserve for the long pleasurable night, could I?) Mahmoud welcomed us with that toothless grim that never failed to arouse my ire. His eyes looked shifty and his lips were pulled back. With his balding head and sunken cheeks, he looked like a perfect Makonde curving in an art gallery. I wondered what the mocking smile was about.

'Allahuakbar' I said.
'Akbar Allah' they mumbled a chorus. I noticed that they were five old ladies and three old men. If the push came to a shove, they would be no match.
'Ismail Dan Fodio bin Batuta,' Mahmoud began, 'it is the injunction of the prophet that on the night of marriage, a maiden virginity be proven. Aisha's mother will present you with a white skin on which you will lie on. After you have finished, these four will take that sheet and present it to her. Then we will see what she is'
'You mean....'
'I have not finished.' Mahmoud said. 'These women will be with you in the tent to ensure that the bloodstains from the mat came from penetration'. I caught my breath suddenly. Looks of ...were exchanged by my tormentors.

'This,' I started talking, slowly articulating every syllable 'is my wife.' I felt Aisha flinch. 'I will not allow you or anyone to interfere in my relationship with her.'

'This is Uthman's daughter' Mahmoud replied harshly. 'I will not think she can be stupid enough to turn her back on ancient practice.'

'I will.' cried Aisha. 'Leave us alone or I will go away with him and never come back!'

I was startled for I didn't expect Aisha to talk like that. Women in this culture are timid and hardly talk in the presence of men. I wondered where Aisha had plucked the courage from.

'Then,' Mahmoud said, deliberately, 'I curse both of you and order you to leave the camp immediately, you and your prostitute! I bunched my fists and lunged for Mahmoud but Aisha quickly caught me from the back. I felt her breasts pricking my back and I mellowed immediately. We folded my tent and camping equipment in the wee hours and headed towards the East.

Knowing me so well, you must be thinking that immediately we left the camp, I jumped on Aisha in our new found freedom. But this freedom in itself was a form of imprisonment. First, I did not intend to get children with Aisha since I knew they would make breaking the marriage difficult. My supply of condoms was enough to take care of that difficulty. And now Aisha in her naiveté of believing in my love had decided to part with them and join my side. You can do anything except abandon your comrade. Irene, you must know that it was a defining moment; a moment when all my wayward tendencies had to be curbed and I engaged myself in a soul searching. I decided that for her life sacrifice to cling unflinchingly on me, Aisha was in love and I felt what I needed to reciprocate.

I noticed a ray of light from our destination as we paced, engaging ourselves in soul searching and thought the sun was about to rise. Then I realized that its trajectory was erratic, and because it was accompanied by some laboured sound, I concluded that it must be a government Land rover since their vehicles were never in good repair.

The Land rover came to a halt in front of us and out jumped my friend Tom. Inside was the newly posted District Commissioner. Fares Suleiman, his driver and two Administration Policemen carrying rifles.

From the greetings and introduction, I noticed that my wife Aisha was looking like a trapped rabbit, and the DC fixed her with a fierce if not contemptuous look. I wondered what bee was in Suleiman's shirt but before I could embark on a fact-finding he asked me a trifle sharply:
'What's her name?'
'Aisha Uthman.' I answered promptly.

Then Tom said to me: 'I am sorry to be the bearer of bad tidings, but Aisha, I am told, had been married before in the city where she attended school. Her husband died of what was suspected to be a case of AIDS. Now Suleiman had been her next suitor and even paid dowry for her, but before they could get down to any business, he heard the suspicion that the girl may be infected. So he insisted and together with Uthman and the girl, they boarded a lorry for Nairobi where four tests were done on her. Two tests were positive and two others were negative. So they still had an impasse. So they agreed on one last test. They had to submit the blood sample to a new research lab and left before the results were out.

Suleiman went to the land rover to get an envelope he waved nay wielded in Aisha's face.
'The result was positive'. Tom continued 'And now the marriage will be dissolved and Uthman compelled to return the bride wealth. I tell you this only because you are my friend.' He concluded.
My dear Irene, you can imagine how I stood there numb for a long time. I started asking myself what if I'd done it. Would the condoms have helped? Then I looked at Aisha and saw the pathos was it the bathos? – registered in her face. I saw the writing on the wall for our relationship the same time she saw it. We were finished.

And now I must tell you why I write. I want to marry you. But don't get me the answer now. I am coming home soon after my tour of duty in

35

December and we will discuss it. I wish also to inform you that I regained my Christian faith.

EVENTS; A DIARY

I don't normally keep a diary, though I own one or two.

SATURDAY 16 MAY, 1994

3 pm – BB Estate: Came Friday to visit two friends – renting an extension. One at Kenya School of Law – doesn't work. The other, medical school. Lecturers' strike over unionisation – final semester suspended; works meanwhile at M. Estate C. Clinic. Some money to get by.

Nothing remarkable this day. But the latter's fiancée arrives. Remember an advert seen on cinema guide: WHITE MISCHIEF!

Oxymoron?

3.20 pm My 'Doctor' friend leaves BB for M-appointment with patient.

4.30 pm – Leave BB in company of the 'lawyer' and the Doctor's fiancée. To meet with the Doc' at Kenya C..

5.00 pm -meet in front of Commerce House. Book tickets.

5.20 pm –White Mischief.

I had read the book of the same title by James Fox. But words don't live. I have also read books like SCARLET AND BLACK – Stendal; Tom Jones – Henry Fielding and more. But this film shocks. Depraved people have a class of their own. Judge them by their standards.

Josslyn Hays – Lord Errol (Joss) tells Diana (D) at her first 'Social' gathering in the colony: 'I want to fuck you!' Lady D is shocked, surprised, bewildered and flabbergasted.

I agree with her.

In form two I learnt some things called 'Osmosis', 'Diffusions'. 'Stupid! People are making a racket about exchanging tickets.

Hawkers pass along the aisles.

Yes, Somehow these things still work, Human beings are in a vacuum. They infect one another and they become the same. Kaput. Airborne diseases. Waterborne germs.

Broughton (Jock) – taciturn if calculating. The neglected though increasingly relevant husband. Money, Crime and Punishment 'Dounia' recalled? The criminal, believing in himself, laughing at the community he lives in, yet being so instrumental, Karamazovs?

D. gives in finally. Not that she has been pursued. Joss only flaunts his wares with recklessness. The mixture of adventure. Is D. fulfilling her dreams about Africa? I forget the details. As the party – the first – a lady

37

asks at D'S sight: what do we have here?' Her consort replies: 'A new piece of meat.' You've seen how meet is treated. It can even stink.

Sex-swap parties were they at Lady Idina's? Lots are cast by women. You get a partner every night. Your 'husband' goes with another. All in good faith. The whites were, of course, a decent lot. They were civilised. Proliferation of sex. Morality. Black servants thought them behaving like goats.
Broughton publicity gives D. up. A feat I can't undertake.
Lord Errol shot. A flower buds in the morn, dies at sundown. Trial. Jock in dock. Jock acquitted. Miserable life with D. Shooting 'accident'.

The lady that goes to see Joss on the cold slab of the mortuary. Such a vitality dead? She must part with a bit of musk. Masturbates in public. Feels the throes she would with Joss. Her finger digs out her woman moistures – musk, smears on Errol's lips. Heartbroken, goes away.
Jock (?) sends a letter for the body – bury it with the body Gwaldys Delemare with her antics. Joss is out of it all. Kaput. One thing must always happen. Affirms this is no madness.
6.30 pm Film over, Escort Doc's fiancées to NO. 11.
7.00 pm – what to do? The Doc needs a drink. Arturo? No, too expensive to get drunk at Karumaindo first - twenty shilling differences in the prices of beer, then later top up at Arturo. Good thinking. Let's go.
Too much noise, vehicles moving. To be continued tomorrow.
Time 8.55 pm.
8.55 pm was this the time the diary stopped? The point in action?
9.00 pm – Monday 19, February 1996. Do let's record (for Saturday 16 May 1994).
7.30 pm – we cross the road. Slink into Karumaindo. Darkness. Grime. Slime. Tang of cigarette, and musk. Musty, if nasty. You stumble on the first stair and reel. Bodies impatiently squeeze past you. Red neon hangs at the head of the stairs like an ulcer. Perforated dim.
Grip the railing. Smooth, wet. Smell your hand. Nose can't place the smell. Two bodies block the stairs. One pushes on the other backed on the railings in a kind of kwasakwasa rhythm. Which dance is this? O the smell of

musk! They are having it out. Wait! His teeth are bared in a grin. Move nearer. It is the snarl of rictus.

He moves on. He moves on. From her purse like a clairvoyant the girl produces a kerchief. One graceful motion and he is wiped clean.

- I Pass. She beckons. A smile like a cats plays on her lips painted red. She says: you'll find it normal and leave your folly. Come new convert. No offerings to leave at the altar, your sins I'll suck away!

- Move on. What a wall covering. The peeling paint peeps shyly from behind sweating bodies rubbing against the wall in rhythm. Unreal. Pervert.

- Level with the weak neon. The noisy hard bar. The juke strikes up a zilizo.

- No table. No standing space. Only rubbing space. The stale sweat, the pale reek of beer. The putrid stench of urine. The market place din. Human wares garishly flaunted.

- P. – The doc' gulps down his first beer. G. and I, we stand staring at hard faces. Remorseless. Seeking no sympathy.

- A snake comes and twines her fingers round my neck. I almost jump. Garden of Eden. O Sodom! Gomorrah!

- Go to the urinal for relief. Sweet escape. But wow! Couples in any imaginable and improbable positions slug it out. A cat smiles at me, inviting from behind the shoulders of another man. Brown teeth. One broke, a tired promise and call. Next please.

- The hard enter, pee and go away. I stand and stare – transfixed. A man enters, pees and takes on a cat who has just wiped her_____.
  In a simple gesture she seems to dismiss the forerunner – fool! This time turns her backside. She grips the creaking cistern for sexual traction.

- Like a somnambulist I stagger away from sight too beautiful to behold. Human being at their barest – basest.

- A leg shoots out. I stagger and crash into my friends. Started, they follow my wake. Curses of our mothers' '...' fill the air. A few week jabs thrown our way. A lit reefer lands on my hair, singeing. One fruitcake attempts to jab G. with a needle he was about to sink on the arms of a girl. She cries out in frustration – an altercation

39

ensues. Drunken din. Crooked coquettish smiles. A near riot at the departure of three strong males.

'Njeri – uliwapatia?'

'No Losi, man feel better than this.' She lifts her skirt, no. Big belt. Underneath, the skin had lost tenderness. Your guess is right. There's no panty. It is open sesame. Broadway.

- Down, down and down we fled. Stumbling on couples. – Some disengaging disgorged tumescence's, shinning predatorily, beginning to flag.
- We burst into the street, dazed. The hurrying Nairobian's were startled, momentarily. Some nodded their heads with understanding. I took many lungful's of air. My mind began to clear. But smell hung around me like guilt itself.

8.30 pm – the clock next to KENCOM says. I looked at each of my two friends. I took off without a by your leave and jumped on a mat for KU.

Postscript.

On 10 Jan, 1995, I boarded a matatu with Njeri at about 6.00 pm. I could not have recognised her as she came in at Githurai, but for the tired smile and peculiar pout of her lips.

SACRIFICES

Pastor Cornelius was ordained deacon of the Church of Pentecost of Kenya in 1985. He was a son of a catechist who also doubled up as the village teacher, Nicanor Watta who had left the Catholic Church and married instead of finishing the course at the Seminary and being admitted to priesthood. While Fr. O'Connor had thought he was bringing up a man of God who will take the church far, Nicanor had seen Beautiful Delilah who was one of the choir members and had fallen hopelessly in love. One evening after choir practice, he had left the seminary for a rendezvous with Delilah, never to go back. Years later, Nicanor was to join with other friends to found the Church of Pentecost of Kenya but he did not seek leadership positions. He believed that his calling was in teaching. It was therefore a befitting surprise that his son would join priesthood and maybe one day become a bishop. He was giddy with elation when his son graduated from Bible College without an incident and his ordination was planned. He knew his son could not make reckless decisions. He was proud.

Cornel was the complete opposite of his father or represented what his father had wanted to be. He was shrewd, calculating and rarely let his feelings show. He believed in moderation. The only indulgence people saw was to ensure that he had his priestly attire to be just right. He was very smart and well turned out and dressed according to religious seasons.

The attraction of the church had been the many rituals that were done by priests. Baptism to him was a mystifying experience, and he often wondered whether the others felt a change inside. He felt quite empty, didn't actually know his feelings. Then there was the Holy Eucharist where they consumed the flesh and blood of Christ. He thought that the first time he would receive Holy Communion there would be some rapture. After raptly following the priest's incantations, the wafers melted in his mouth and the 'Blood of Christ' had a tangy taste. After the service, the priest asked him to the vestry and directed him to finish what was left in the chalice as it had been blessed. He did as he was told and did not contort his face.

There was a warm feeling as the liquid, in larger quantities went down his throat and he realised he was feeling giddy. He profusely thanked the priest for the honour and asked the priest to recommend him for training for priesthood. During the church elders meeting later on, the priest duly proposed his name and he was accepted enthusiastically.

The Bible College was a good distraction and he loved his theology. He learnt that there was no God and he then learnt that there was God. Some of the things that he learnt shocked him.

At one point he almost left the Bible College because he could not reconcile to what he was being taught and what he was reading. Some of it would be seditious- were clearly blasphemous. Then he realised that the course was designed in a way that he would gain his spirituality and be strong in his faith. He had not known that even some of the saints went through self-doubt, and that there were so many different thought patterns within the Christian communion. He understood completely why there were many schisms, and how this led to many religious sects and he understood that the Church of Pentecost in Kenya, his own church, was a result of such thoughts. He wondered why exactly they had broken from the Catholic Church and he thought that they must have been looking for pride. Or was it control? Was it style of worship?

Having gone through a catholic sponsored school, he saw no major differences between the Church of Pentecost in Kenya and the catholic liturgy and worship. His father did not fit this pattern. He made a mental note to analyse the other founders of his church. Maybe then, he will look at father more kindly. He knew his father had left the seminary but that was the end of it. The subject was never discussed. He had often thought that maybe it was because he wanted to marry and he knew that as a priest in the Catholic Church, this was not going to be possible. Now his church welcomed marriage but he could not know why his father never rose to become more than a catechist. Well, he had his ideas and marriage was not one of them. He knew his father would be surprised.

Now, the Catholic Church was an intriguing one. History is very clear that the holy fathers used to marry and some had concubines with whom they sired children. There seems to be no theological sanction in not marrying or marrying. Could it be that the church was worse off when popes used to marry? This was a very doubtful thing.

As far as Cornelius was concerned, the same problems that bedevilled the church today had done so in the past. Nothing, it seems, and the Old Testament says, will change. Everything that happens now had happened in the past. Some of those popes who married were effective and in many cases wielded immense political power. Some because of relations through marriage, and other Popes were powerful because of their charisma. Of recent, Pope John Paul II was so powerful that he dislodged communism from Poland and most of Eastern Europe.

When he started working, he was posted to a rural area. The Bible school had adequately prepared him and he was ready to meet with the challenges he found himself in. He discovered fast that the people came to the church because many wanted to reaffirm their faith in divine existence. He could not believe how many disbelievers flocked the church and wondered- how did Moses persevere all those years in the wilderness with recalcitrant population until he gave the mantle to Joshua? He was able to harvest souls, but he also lost others. But he had the time. He knew that he had to be determined, persistent and consistent for people to understand and come round to the ways of the lord. He never thought he would completely defeat the doubt in people's heads so he gave them chances for discussion. He never forced anyone to come to give their lives to God. Indeed he never made even one alter call and the elders were very unhappy.

To compromise so as to harvest souls to Christ as they called it, after he preached- and he did preach a powerful sermon- one of the senior pastors in a deep and knowing voice would come to ask the congregation to come to the lord and confess. People came in droves and confessed. He realised the power of his word and bid his time.

It is in counselling though, that he excelled and he felt more fulfilled. He did counsel so many parishioners with myriad problems, the most intriguing being marriage counselling; it made him decide not to marry. Most people that he had very high opinion of had been made desperate by trivia. And some trivia made good people of the lord desperate and empty in their souls.

There was this woman he wedded with a young business man in a glittering wedding ceremony. After the honeymoon in Seychelles, she came back and threw him the wedding ring and asked Pastor Cornelius to return it to the alleged husband. She didn't think there was anything important in the marriage and the man had not seemed to know what to do with a woman, and she was not going to stay in that slavery called marriage. Why? Can you imagine, he even refused to undress when the lights were on and even when they were switched off he only removed the trouser and shirt and firmly remained with his vest and boxers. I tried to touch him and he said bad manners! I was burning hot and getting wet and here was Jesus reincarnated! Oomph! I tried to sooth him and run my fingers lightly on his face, back and when I tried to touch where he matters, there was a little limp thing and then he told me to kneel down we pray. He spent the night cursing the devil and saying that I should be cured! Well I went to the toilet and cured myself and sobbed as I was doing it. He stood just outside the toilet shouting *'Riswa!' 'Riswa!'* Well pastor, return him the ring. So what happened next? I decided to not flog a dead snake. I tried to pleasure myself but you see, when you have a banana that has turned yellow and yet it's not ripe, you can't eat it. Can you, Good pastor? Of course- yes- no…er…., I mean it depends. Depends on what pastor? I need my groove. Return the ☺☹🕯ring. Okay sis… let's not be so hard on yourself, let's pray over it. No more prayers pastor and I am not your sister by any stretch of imagination. Show me a hard on and I will respect you. Hey sis this is a church compound.

Useless, you are just like him. Well go wed him with that ring then. And she fled, left the pastor Cornel in a bind. That was his first hard case, and he designed a pre-counselling questionnaire form just to be sure that he got to know what to expect with a client and he has never gotten a nasty fright since then. Nowadays, he got amused, saddened or just perplexed with how human minds worked and how relations were wrecked. He thought of the many walking 'nut' cases. Sometimes he thought that they confessed so as to tempt his mettle.

Some people wanted to become violent when he explored areas that they wanted to hide, or when he refused to give them an answer, tell them what to do. Almost all wanted him to agree to prejudiced positions so that they wouldnot be responsible for their actions. They would say 'the pastor told me'. Just like when he preached certain sermons he was sure to get quoted in homes for people to get their way. Men liked the quote 'women, obey your husbands…' And women loved the part '…men, love your wives'.

The world was virtually crazy. Sometimes the counselling sessions would get so dicey. Unrequited women and young girls sent by the devil himself knocked at his door. In his small office that served as the vestry, he had started counselling by both the client and him sitting in front of his desk, facing each other in a relaxed atmosphere. He even served the client's water, some biscuits or sweets to make them comfortable. He engaged in small talk to make them comfortable. One girl, a daughter to one of his worshippers came in with other things in her mind. She pretended that she didn't know she was wearing a short skirt and proceeded to show the pastor her thighs, and was just there smiling and looking foolish. It was her idea of seduction, and the response was instantaneous. The pastor stopped breathing and choked on his words. She saw her chance and came to the pastor and started fondling him, confessing her love.

Cornelius was very overcome with her embrace and touches that he found himself ejaculating. This is what saved him from utter ruin. He changed his mien and asked the girl that they pray and admonished the devil. He told the girl not to blame herself. Satan was walking everywhere, looking for people that he may devour, and what had happened was one of the ways that Satan worked.

Then there was this wife of a teacher he had been counselling. They were undergoing sessions as a couple but this time she came to see him alone.

He asked where the teacher was but he was told he had travelled for drama competition with his students.

The lady herself was a housewife and he had been trying to touch the source of their differences for the past one month, and they kept skirting around the issues. She took some biscuits and was very direct with the pastor. She told the pastor that the reason she had opted for counselling was to be near him and she wanted to really make love to him as the teacher did not satisfy her. She offered to be doing general work in his compound and no one will be the wiser when they did their thing. He said no and she insisted, held him and kissed him profusely. He took his hand and guided it to touch her core. She had no pant. Wet and hot. She said that she would scream 'rape!' unless they did it. It was just too much. He agreed to finger her, telling her of terrible diseases and that if they were to do it, they had to have a condom. When she came, she shuddered and then suddenly lolled her head against his chest. He thought she was going to faint, nay, die on him. This was the last time he ever did any counselling in that relaxed posture. Now, he would sit behind his desk, and leave the door slightly ajar so that the counselee knew where things stood. He also had a bell to summon his clerk, a boy who had done form six and was waiting to join university, at the faintest sign of trouble.

All things considered, Cornelius realised that he was only human and some needs had to be fulfilled. At first, he started by masturbating but he soon realised that God did not quite create people to fire their own guns. It gave him momentary relief, and it felt phoney. He realised that he must get the real thing, the real experience. He thought back to his youth, when he was growing up.

When he grew too old to sleep in his parent's bed, he started sharing a room with his aunt. When he was ten, he started realising that the aunt would take him to the bathroom with her, wash him, and bathe quite freely, especially when there was no one at home. She also used to sleep naked and hold him. She was so warm that he used to fall asleep immediately. They got attached. In his sleep, he used to feel like he was being touched, and one day, he woke up to find that he was between the legs of his aunt.

46

By the age of thirteen, he and the aunt had a little secret- they were having sex and no one was the wiser. Then the aunt told him that she was going away and he was not to tell, as she would come back and they would play the games again. The next he heard was that she was now married to a pastor of the same church serving in a place called Naivasha. He felt a profound loss and from that day, the idea of becoming a pastor slowly started planting in his head. He felt that if he had to become a pastor to enjoy the little games, so be it. Aunt Margaret came to visit after about eight months but she was heavily pregnant and looked quite ugly. He lost the desires and even when he was alone with her felt nothing. He felt a little betrayed but he still had love for her. He felt that he would become a pastor just to show her that he was worthy.

He wondered always what was wrong with people. When he went to high school, another boy started fondling him. He was so enraged he pushed away the boy and told him he would knife him next time. From that moment he carried with him a pen knife and was very untrusting with all men. He just thought it was dirty for a man to sleep with a man and wondered where someone would insert his penis. Then he realised it would be the anus or the mouth and he got more revolted. The thought led him to vomit his breakfast.   He decided that life was better lived the way that it appeared to have been planned, and to be less of a change agent. After all, what was there to change? He got excited with his aunt, then his aunt had to marry and he didn't want to complicate his life. He rejected homosexuality. But he was only human and decided that apart from masturbating, he will have to do something about the raging fires that were kept hidden by the cloth, especially when he faced the congregation. Thank God for the design of Priestley garb.

He knew getting to flesh joints may be a tall order and he had to be very careful. He knew full well that marriage was a bore, particularly sex became boring and people got troubled for no reason. And also, before he was ordained, this disease called AIDS had reared its ugly head...

Now and then he needed to go to a town where he would be anonymous or he had to create another character. He decided that Nakuru town fitted the bill. Nairobi was so cosmopolitan and the chances of being found out he thought were higher. To reach Nakuru, he would leave his rural parish along Kisumu - Busia road and take Mbukinya bus and drop off at Kericho. In Kericho town, he would get into a petrol station loo and change into snazzy clothes, complete with a cap. The transition left the good pastor Cornelius Odawo at the Esso petrol station and out emerged Jimmy Oraro as he was known in Nakuru. He would then book another bus bound for Nairobi but alight in Nakuru. In Nakuru, he would go straight to KANU Street. This was the street named after baba na mama. The president was the all-powerful Moi, and he looked indestructible and KANU itself looked like the ruling party for the next millennia. This was a stomping ground of KihikaKimani and Kariuki Chottara. Wa! There was order here.

Gituamba literally on the main highway had bragging rights of the flesh trade but KANU Street provided more wonders. There was this joint that offered all wonders of the world. Pole dances and lap dances and sex at a fee. He liked the lap dances more. One, he had no chance of getting a disease; he was more free to sample and he liked the moment they trained their asses to his face. Woi! It was glory redefined. God created a swell world with all wonders and at such times, he felt there should be no heaven apart from what was on earth. At this time he forgot the repression Moi and KANU regime meted on Kenyans. He almost forgave them. But he could not tell the flock when getting a permit to hold a harambee for improvement of the church building had not been granted since the guest of honour was to be an opposition leader.

On his way from Kericho, he would become talkative and would chat up the person sitting next to him, to get the feeling of being ordinary. He knew that people put up a show when they saw pastors and the truth was not in them. He usually took night buses and particularly liked chatting up ladies. Occasionally, night bus romance, with its limitations had been experienced. One time it made him pass his real destination, Nakuru and he had to plead with the driver to drop him at Gilgil police roadblock. He sweet talked the police to put him on a bus back to Kisumu. He left behind

48

a disappointed fellow traveller who had enjoyed his attention and baffled bus driver who knew all his passengers were destined for Nairobi. At least the manifest said so. Tough luck. Next time baby.

One day, he found a'mzungu' man seated in his corner. The DJ had a great respect for Jimmy as he was a heavy tipper and the payments he made to the girls also reached DJ Jesus. Jesus! How did this DJ land on this as a name? Anyway, the *mzungu* welcomed him and they were soon talking.

The white man told him that he was an engineer- which was true but he did not reveal that he was also Reverend Father John McDonald, originally from Tampa, Florida in the USA. At that time, he was attached to the local Catholic Church but was also doing some work for CIA. Life, as Father McDonald later told him, was complicated. What he told Jimmy was that they were rehabilitating Naivasha Nairobi road. He actually worked there advising the local engineers who he found competent enough and he trawled various social places to 'get whispers from the ground'. Jimmy said he was a businessman buying bales of used clothes and selling in Busia. He thought that if he said he was a teacher, the way he had been telling people, the engineer may judge him in a single trajectory. But the engineer, man of God and sleuth knew that Jimmy was lying. He told Jimmy to his face, and asked Jimmy which church he ministered in. The glass in Jimmy's hand slipped and fell on the floor with its contents and it was prevented from breaking because of the heavy carpet.

The engineer was very solicitous, picked up his glass and told him sorry again and again for being so thoughtless and bought him two fingers of Johnny Walker, and added a double before speaking again. Being an older man, he was very aware that the pastor often came here and never expected anyone to find him out. The pastor must be feeling that his career was over.

Sorry pal, I didn't mean to offend. You see, I do other jobs apart from engineering. If it would make any difference to you, I am also a pastor, I am Reverend Father John MacDonald, and I serve in the Catholic Church. What! Jimmy asked, jaw dropping. Yes, we are all human, son and I don't blame you. You see here in Africa, you have so much pretence. For me

49

even at home I go to pubs and hot spots like this. That way, my faith grows and I serve my parishioners better. I am able to experience the same things they go through and sometimes I succumb, just like them.

When one comes to the confessional, I am able to understand so completely they are always amazed. I take them through the steps of how they sinned and they wonder how I knew. I am proud I have changed so many women and men for the better- at a very small sacrifice on my part. What? Have you ever considered the price Jesus had to pay in order to save mankind? God that he was is and will be- amen! He agreed to become man! Jimmy brightened up. This man was dynamite! An older theologian, a man of God like him had opened his eyes in a flash and he could at once see that he was not a sinner himself. He had to do these things so that he could understand the passion of Christ. Jesus- I like the name Jesus and I think I like the DJ. Just then, the DJ belted

I'll see you when we meet there… in the valley of the shadow of death. He remembered Bony M's 'By the rivers of Babylon, there we sat down and there we wept…' The only record closest to secular music his father kept.

I told you that I do many jobs. I am a priest but I also went to school to do engineering, and this earns money for my order and me. MacDonald continued. But I am also involved with government agencies. I look for information and pass on to security agencies. They use the information to track bad people, arrest them and prosecute them. The only agreement is that I am never to be called to testify on anything. Information supplied by me has helped avert disasters, save lives. I am proud of my life and I think so should you, pastor, troubled as you are. He stopped and Jimmy agreed with him completely. You are a bright young man. What you lack are opportunities.

They drunk, danced chatted and pawed girls into the early hours of the morning. They were inseparable and when MacDonald dropped Jimmy at a backstreet hotel to rest, he promised to come back and take him to Nakuru National Park that afternoon. Jimmy felt very ecumenical.

As they drove through the park, they would pause to take pictures of various animals that Jimmy had only seen their pictures.

As the sun set, it was time for the big cats to come out, the hunters, the boys. He was frightened when they encountered a pride of lions but MacDonald told him to relax. They even saw the shy leopard stretched on a branch, and only the trained eyes could see his majesty with the help of a telescope that MacDonald had in the car. They drank some whisky that was in the car and he gained more and more confidence. His more experienced mate cautioned him and prevented any disaster. For instance, he felt an urge to urinate and wanted to get out of the car and MacDonald had to pint out for him the sigh that said they should not come out of the car at that point.

Five people had been attacked by predators at that very point, and lost their lives. They then went for supper, and Jimmy discussed his thoughts and aspirations with MacDonald. The Reverend saw an opportunity of developing a young like-minded man who may be grateful to him in future and decided to get him into a college to do a Master's degree in America. They went out and indulged again and then Jimmy had to go and turn into Cornelius Odawo, the good and adorable pastor.

Father MacDonald said not to worry, he will pay for the air ticket and first semester fees and Cornelius need only raise money for upkeep, then he will be fixed onto some work study programmes. The fact that the college was a catholic one was not discussed did not appear important and never mattered.

Back to his parish, he shared with his father who has always been his advisor without appearing so.
His father was overjoyed. He presented his proposal to the Parish council and they passed it and recommended him to the Bishop of the diocese for release to study. In his absence, a curate would be employed.

Once he received a letter of offer from the St. Joan's Seminary in Florida, an air ticket and a recommendation for visa, all that remained was clearance from his lordship. The bishop's secretary, a stern looking and matronly woman in her fifties asked him to wait.

From 8.am, he waited till about 4pm when the secretary told him that his lordship wished to see him. He had been keeping a careful distance from the bishop as he knew that a moth died by moving too near to the light. He was careful and did everything with moderation, not being entirely colourless and not being too noticed. Everyone agreed that he was a dedicated and conscientious worker. Now Bishop Silas was getting old.

Having led the 'rebels' that founded the Church of Pentecost in Kenya, he was easily appointed the bishop. There was consensus and no election. Now he was old and his compatriots were also old.

Nicanor was a good five years younger but then he had refused to be a priest, and preferred being a school teacher, and a catechist. He was now a good church elder. The others who had become priests like Silas lacked imagination, and having gotten into priesthood just wanted the trappings of power and harassed him to be named Rural Deans, Archdeacons, Assistant Bishops, Canons etc. their demands were as ceaseless as they were irritating, and he had had to give in and now he could not give any other position except that of the Bishop.

When they started, they had not thought of the title Primate or Archbishop. He personally did not want pomposity, and so he had decided not to bring this at the top decision making organ of the church, the Pentecostal Church of Kenya Council. Now, he saw a young man who was obviously bright and very well behaved, a son to Nicanor whom he had the greatest admiration for.

From the time the secretary had told him of the visitor and the nature of the request, he had simply asked for the application documents and told the secretary to tell him to wait. He wanted to call a fellow Bishop from one of the independent churches for advice, and the Principal of the Bible College where all their pastors trained for advice. The secretary reminded him that the telephone had been 'cut' two months ago, and it could not be paid for as there were no funds in the church accounts. And yet his Archdeacons always had money- they retained money collected so that they could leverage him, the bishop, a Vicar of Christ.

Bishop Silas' only option was to read the Bible and meditate an old trick he had perfected in his long stint as the overall prelate. It always worked and sometimes like on this case, it had to be moved along by stiff glasses of church wine that he kept handy. At such times, his eyes became blood shot and when he looked you in the eye, you could not hide the truth from him. People never liked meeting him when he had kept you in the bench for long before calling you in for a meeting. He was a hard man to impress. Cornelius Odawo had heard of these rumours but he was unperturbed. He was not as implicated as other pastors. Others dipped their hands into the offertory baskets, others comforted lonely and spurned women, and others could not control their urge for the bottle. He was an exception, he believed. He entered the Bishops Opulent Office- it was a large office, huge desk, many crosses of different sizes and verses written in gold and hung in strategic places.

The Bishop did not rise or say anything. Cornelius just stood inside the door and looked anywhere but at the Bishops searching gaze. He was eventually told to sit. He could see the bishop sweating a little, like he was flushed as well. Now young man, tell me your mission, the Bishop intoned, as if he wanted to deliver a homily. Cornelius relaxed instantly. Father in Christ, I have through sheer luck and Gods doing got this chance to study at St. Joan's Seminary in Florida.

I chanced upon a white priest, John MacDonald who had a sick person in hospital, he invited me to go and help him pray and after we prayed, the patient got better.

He was discharged the next day and reverend MacDonald was so impressed, he straight away offered to help me find a place to further my studies so that I could serve my church better. I now beg for your indulgence, lordship to approve of me to go, and I can promise you I will come back and serve God with even more vigour. And what, pray are you going to study? Well, Lordship I thought you would advise on that. Ah! This is good. I would very much like someone to study canon law. Canon law, Bishop Silas repeated, nodding his head greatly. I need someone who can design a structure for our church so that things are clear. You know I am getting old, and everyone else is. I don't want that when my time comes to go rest with the lord, people turn on each other like I see in many churches. I want things to be clear so that I rest easy in my grave. Thank you Lordship makes perfect sense and it is an area I will enjoy. Well, young man, if you could send me the outline of the structure, I can give you advice so that you produce a good report. Thank you.

The Bishopthen rose and indicated that the meeting was over then came round and escorted him to the door. Cornelius realised that alcohol fumes covered the Bishoplike a halo. Well, young man, be careful of the women there. I would like to preside over your wedding in our church here. Many have gone to that land and never come back. They become slaves to white women who dazzle them and lead them away from the lord. You are the son to my friend and I trust that he brought you up well. You can wait and pick your letter. Call me the secretary.

Armed with a passport where he was down as Reverend Cornelius Odawo, and his profession was put down as priest, a letter from the college, a visa and a huge ambition, Cornelius left his parishioners amid great sadness and elation from both sides. They loved him and wanted him to stay but they were also proud that he was going to America to study. No priest in their church had achieved such a feat. He was giddy with triumph but wondered if he would deliver the expectations of many people: his father, his parishioners, his Lordship, John MacDonald, his benefactor. The list could be extended.

His first time to board an aeroplane, he never showed any sign of nervousness. He was modest and looked at what seasoned travellers were doing and he copied them without appearing to do so. They had to take a connecting flight from Seattle but this time he had made friends who shared the same row with him and they guided him through it all. John was waiting at the local airport and took him to his new abode. Then they went for supper and he went back to his room, agreeing with John that he wouldbe picked the next day for orientation.

When he looks back now, America was like a blur. A good student and keen scholar, Cornelius distinguished himself and was fast tracked for a PhD programme. A man of his words, he had been giving drafts to Bishop Silas and they had agreed that the position of a Bishop had to be held by a person who had at least a master's degree or higher. He must have served for fiveyears or more in a rural parish. To avoid unnecessary competition, the church had to form a search committee with Lay persons and pastors in equal number. They had to be elected from all the congregations. The committee's role was to advice those they thought qualified to apply and then they would interview the person at a special session. Apart from his sessions on KANU street, there was only one other matter that happened in America that he never wanted anybody to know.

One time, John came with another man that he introduced as John Burris. He told Cornelius that Burris was his case officer and wanted to talk to him. He left them and promised to come back after two hours so that they could both go for lunch. John Burris did not waste time. He explained to Cornelius that a case officer was a controller of a spy. He had recruited and trained John MacDonald on intelligence gathering and all information from John passed through him and him alone. He had come to recruit Cornelius for training. He stressed that there was no chance of refusing the offer as the recruitment had started when he met Father MacDonald.

Where did the admission, the fees, the air ticket and the visa come from? I can tell you for fact that it was my unit's job. Cornelius saw everything now in perspective. He had wondered if the one time he prayed for MacDonald's parishioner in hospital is what did the trick, just like that. He will never believe in magic wands anymore.

Anytime you will not obey what I tell you, I have very good colour pictures and videos of you at that club in Nakuru. I am sure you know DJ Jesus? Sweat started pouring out of Cornelius pores. He shifted and then John Burris assured him: we don't intend to use them unless you deviate from the script. It's called insurance my boy. With that he produced many papers from his briefcase and gave Cornelius places to put his signature. He was given a training schedule.

At lunch, it was difficult to know if Father MacDonald knew what went on. Burris had warned him against discussing any information with another person even if in the same unit, unless they have been given a group assessment. This was to protect member of the unit and the unit as a whole. He enjoyed a sumptuous lunch washed down with expensive wine. After all, he was an expense item for the unit. He trained for six months and after graduation where he was introduced to other members (he assumed) of the unit. MacDonald never appeared there but he was called at the end that there was a car waiting for him. Inside was MacDonald and a woman he didn't recognise and who did not offer a handshake or name.

Two months after training and as he was preparing for graduation and departure home, he was called by the St. Joan's Rector, Bishop Arthur O'Neal. He was told that he had to be ordained there and then as a catholic priest. He was stunned. He asked why and the Bishop reminded him that members of the unit obeyed orders from superiors. It slowly sank on him. He was trapped. Bishop O'Neal assured him that his bishop will not know, and that in any he was soon to be bishop of his church. He was trained not to ask questions and he repressed the words that he nearly uttered.

After the ceremony, he went to the loo. On coming out, the bishop was coming in and told him that there was a rogue unit member that needed controlling. He was to shift his major activities to Naivasha and open a church there. Fund for building the church would be availed.

After nearly four years out of the country, he came back to find a church that had undergone several changes, and needed some quick fixes and longer term planning. Some of his parishioners no longer worshipped at the church. Some had transferred to new stations and a few had died. Yet others just drifted away. The tithe was low. The Bishop had come to welcome him from Nairobi and he had booked for both of them a Kenya airways domestic flight to Kisumu. Bishop Silas was very happy. And

Cornelius had been a good dedicated priest, now firmly under his tutelage. The Bishop briefed him and gave him the task of travelling to all churches to study and revive them. The Bishop was happy and told him that he now only survived on the money Cornelius used to send to him from America. He was tired and wanted to retire. He asked for permission to start another church in Naivasha and this was granted.

In all, there were 20 churches and parishes. Each church covered a certain area, and for small worship groups, meetings were held in members' houses. Many members could not reach the main church and so the priest went to give them Holy Communion on site. This was typical of all sites. Offerings and tithe was collected by the priest. He noted all the collections as the bishop had told him to. He stayed in each parish for a week, and got to know Christians. He visited them with the local priest and asked them their opinion on many matters. He was very down to earth and he gained many friends from each congregation he visited. He preached memorable sermons in each church.

At the conclusion of the tour, he wrote a candid report to the bishop. All was not well with the pastors. There needed to be spiritual revivals organised twice a year for pastors to put them back on track. And there needed to be good accountability. The lay members only went to listen to boring services and sermons. And giving out money… They had become disillusioned. They were losing trust in the church hierarchy and were not giving as much as they should. He confirmed what Bishop Silas had suspected all along. He asked for three weeks off, which he proposed to spend in Naivasha to lay groundwork for the new church.

As a catholic priest, he was asked to go and sleep in a mission not far from Naivasha. Later that evening, he saw a hulk of a man and they were introduced. The man was dressed like a hunter and behaved strangely and people avoided him. During supper, he sat next to Cornelius and they introduced each other. Cornelius lied that he trained as a priest in the UK and gave his alibi. It was part of his work. He was to shadow this man until fresh orders arrived. They exchanged contacts and the man left in a noisy pick-up, driving away into the Maasai night, alone.

He left Naivasha after one week and went to Nakuru to see if DJ Jesus still reigned. The first person he spotted was MacDonald, in their old corner, looking cool as if he stayed there all the time, and was not supposed to be in America. He was stunned. And Jesus remembered him. He was mobbed by those who knew him. Then he saw a girl, and he froze, just like that. She was so divinely beautiful and he decided there and then that she would never again dance to the stares of other men. This was going to be his wife. His knees wanted to fail him and he sat down next to his friend and recruiter. He sent for the girl.

Hazel, when she came, thought he wanted a lap dance. He said no, he wanted her to sit with them. He wanted to talk to her. He will pay her charges the whole night. She told her to go dress up. That night, they left the club early and went to his room. He still remembers the delights of that night and he still prides himself for making correct decisions. They agreed that they wouldmeet in Kisumu in a week. He told her that she would no longer dance as he would pay her. If she wanted to dance, she would dance for him.

When he went to Kisumu to see the Bishop, he told his lordship of his nuptial plans and it was agreed that he would introduce the girl to the Bishop that week. Then the Bishop invited him for supper. They made small talk, and also talked about the Bishops retirement. The Bishop told him that he wanted him to take over. They agreed that Cornelius would fund the bishop's travels to elect the search committee. The Bishops wife left for the kitchen after introductions. At one time she called the name Hazel but Cornelius never thought of a thing.

They sat there and they could hear the sound of pots and pans. The bishop's wife came in and greeted him with delight and thanked him for the good work he was doing. She noted that life had improved and they now had many blessings and the Bishop was rejuvenated and happy in his work. Cornel smiled contritely and profusely thanked God and they all said AMEN!

The bishop's wife, Esther she was called, started laying the table. She called out to the kitchen hurry up and mumbled about children needing to be working harder and not malingering. She went to the kitchen and came with a steaming bowl of chicken followed by WHAT! Hazel. The very Hazel that was Cornelius fiancée! Their eyes met and Hazel froze like a mannequin that you see through a glass window, displaying stylish clothes. Cornelius tried to stand and talk and at the same time sit. Esther looked at her daughter and, not having captured the scene well, rushed back to help her daughter whom she thought was about to fall. Bishop Silas surveyed the scene and a foggy idea started forming in his head and he knew that whatever it was, he was right as always. He had prided himself in reading people and he thought now that both his daughter and pastor Cornel were physically attracted to each other and that this was love at first sight. Whoever else he wanted to marry will be shoved aside. This was an opportunity to not only pass the mantle to his trusted friend's son, but also to a son in law. What a way to retire! The best insurance!

He fell on his knees and intoned. Let's pray and they all went down onto their knees, with the plate that Hazel had been carrying put on the next table for convenience, and assuring that Hazel's legs will not give way under her.

The lord of Abraham, Isaac and Jacob… he intoned and then paused. The only true Lord and our spiritual guide, oh eternal father. We stand before thee confused but confident in your wisdom, humble and meek on our own but strong in your power. You have shown your servant, pastor Cornel the direction he needs to take for his lifelong happiness, indeed your miracles will never cease. Cornel my son, Hazel my daughter, may the bolt of lightning that has passed between you be turned into a bold decision of matrimony…what!

Esther hissed. Woman be quiet in the presence of the Lord! Bishop Silas' holy bellow rattled the glasses that had been laid on the table. He continued to pray. These two young people please guide. Us old people, make us proud of their decision for you alone are holy, you alone are to be worshiped, and you alone are to be trusted.

For us mortals, give us eyes to discern your meaning, the humility to realize your grace and the heart to love you and in loving you, spread the message of love to one another, eternally. Amen. Then all said Amen! Cornel, you may greet our daughter, Hazel. Hazel, this is pastor Cornel, and he will be my successor as Bishop of the Pentecostal Church of Kenya. He is my trusted pastor. Cornel, this is my last born daughter. She is the only one yet to marry. She has been educated in Anglican Boarding School in Ng'iya and she passed well and I took her to Loreto. She has recently finished training at Hyridge Teachers College and is yet to be posted. I believe that she should start teaching when she is married but she has not yet met a deserving man, like you. Let's eat before the food gets cold and then you can talk. By the way you don't have to sleep in a hotel. Tonight you will be our guest. Is that so mama? He asked, addressing Esther who by now had started to get wise. She involuntarily said amen, thinking this was an extension of the prayers.

Calm returned and with it a stiff normalcy and Cornel prayed in his hard and thanked God for being so merciful. As the two continued to lay the table, Bishop Silas assured Cornel that he could still change his mind about that other woman. God works in mysterious way, and consider today a miracle. We have brought Hazel up well and you will get a fine wife if you decide that it is her. She likes reading and singing, and she will make a good wife to a bishop. And best if I preside over your wedding before I retire.

He was saved from more enticing advice when Esther called them to the table, and they washed hands. Luckily, he sat next to Hazel, facing her dad and hazel herself was facing her mother. He ate very carefully, not wanting his feelings to be known, but thankful that he would not have to reveal where he had met Hazel. He thought that his reaction on seeing Hazel in their home had been artless. He was better than that stunt he did, and had the old man been observant and not fixated on marrying her daughter off to the right man, he would have been discovered, and it would have been very difficult explaining how and where they met. At that moment, he believed that God works in mysterious ways.

60

After supper, Bishop Silas showed him to his bedroom which was semi-detached from the main house. He told him that they could talk and pray over the matter with Hazel and then they can talk more in the morning. Bishop and Esther then went to sleep, and Hazel took him to his room and for two hours they prayed…

The next morning after breakfast, Cornel asked Bishop Silas if they could talk alone. He then told Bishop that he had prayerfully looked at the matter and was convinced that Hazel was the right woman for him and would like to marry her as soon as banns were published. He wanted to get married before becoming a bishop so that his gospel could be complete. They then agreed to announce this to the two ladies, and went to the sitting room where after fervent prayers, the bishop announced that he had accepted to entertain a request from pastor cornel to wed his last born daughter and asked Esther to say something. Esther was overcome by emotion and as tears cascaded down her plump face, she started singing the Christian anthem *tukute*…

At their next rendezvous with McDonald, he told him of the marriage plans and he approved profusely. He also briefed him on the succession plan, and McDonald agreed that it would be good if he invited the Rector of his former college to attend both his wedding and enthronement as Bishop. They agreed that he discusses with Bishop Silas that his selection as Bishop be done and thereafter his wedding to Hazel to take place before his enthronement so that they could have the mother of the church as it were. They would then go for a honey mood and then come back for enthronement. It was therefore necessary that the team from St. Joan's Seminary be present in Kenya for nearly a month. McDonald said he will handle the invitations.

They were at the Nakuru club till 2 am when McDonald reminded him about the rogue priest, the unit member that he had seen at the mission.

The priest had been seen driving around with a gun around Naivasha and seemed to have been talking to himself a lot and acting suspiciously. He had booked at the Mission, took supper and then left to God knows where. He had his trademark four wheel drive pick-up and had stopped at a bar in Naivasha town and bought some bottles of beer at about 12.30 am. He then went and parked his car at a certain location and kind of settled for the night.

Cornel was the only agent in the area and the task was simple. Drive to the sport and since the priest slept with the gun, could he contrive so that the gun goes off accidentally? He should then search the pick-up truck for any documents of interest the priest had, put in his car, then go to the mission and gain entry to the priests' room and search for other documents and put in the car. By the time he was through, he would pass by the scene and the Kenya police would be there. He had tostop and ask for the investigating officer's name and contacts and bring the same to MacDonald to take over from there. They would then meet at the Midlands Hotel for breakfast, say around 830 am.

When he reached the scene, he passed and parked on the side of the road in some shrubs so that the car that MacDonald had given him, a grey Toyota AE100 which was popular with the working class in Kenya, would not be seen from the road. He then walked back and on reaching the truck, it appeared and indeed was empty. He opened its door which was not secured and took a valise that had some documents and put in the boot of the car. He then came back and was getting convinced that the priest was not around for he could not have climbed the acacia trees that surrounded the area. He heard some grunt and approached carefully.

As MacDonald had told him, the priest lay there, blanket askew and his trademark rifle nearby, the muzzle resting on his chin, just near the duodenum. He looked around. Am I being set up? Has the man killed himself? On the man's left hand, there was a half empty bottle of Jameson. He saw no sign of the beer bottles or cans that MacDonald had told him the man bought.

This man was a total disaster. It was only good that he killed himself, for the unit's safety. Then he saw that even the safety catch of the gun was not on. He approached slowly and with gloved hand supported the weapon-just in the position he found it, and pulled the trigger.

The report was a muffled crack and not a boom that he would have expected in an enclosed place. The bullet must have gone straight through the brain and cut off communication to the limbs which, mixed with alcoholic stupor only produced feeble twitches.

There was no need to do anything else. He had been trained not to leave any sign of his presence in that kind of scene. He relieved the priests limp hand of the bottle of Jameson and walked back to his car and drove to the mission, reaching at six am and headed straight to the priests room where his search revealed nothing. He then went to the receptionist and asked about long term accommodation for ten missionaries from UK in one month's time. He was given the rates. He did tentative booking and the brother who served him invited him to stay for Holy Communion at 7 am and thereafter to breakfast but he said there was a priest he was to pick in Nakuru town and proceed for another service. He got back into the car and drove away, the Jameson having been a good companion as he was feeling warm and on top of things.

There was the inevitable crowd when he reached that junction at 7.30 am and police had formed a cordon. He introduced himself as a priest and immediately, they were interested to know if he could identify the body they had discovered as his passport said that he was a priest. He said yes and no- depending on which order. When they drew away the blanket they had covered him with, he recognized the man alright but showed no sign and denied knowledge of him.

The man had died with a surprised snarl in his face and indeed looked dangerous even in death. He gave the investigating officer the address and phone number to the mission and took his contacts as well. He was careful not to leave his name or address. He drove off to Nakuru.

He found MacDonald sitting unperturbed and reading the days papers. He asked for the car keys and gave them to a waiter, not bothering to ask what

Cornelius had gathered. They had a slow breakfast and then went to sit in MacDonald's room. No word of his mission was discussed: instead, MacDonald seemed more interested in discussing details of his wedding and upcoming enthronement. The other rule in the service was: 'don't offer information not asked of you'.

After finalising the plans, MacDonald led him out and to the car park. There, he was shown a car a Suzuki Vitara and MacDonald gave him the Key and told him to use for his missionary work. He was told the vehicle had an after sales service for 10,000 kilometres and that there was enough cash in the briefcase in the boot to cater for his campaign for selection, his wedding, honeymoon and enthronement. He thanked MacDonald and as he drove back to Kisumu, he wondered how he would break the news to the Bishop. He had not bought a car so as to appear modest. He had made good savings when he was in Florida and could have bought a car if he wanted. He had more that Kshs. 3 million in fixed deposit and this gave him a modest sum every three months which he reinvested. He had also bought land and built a four storey building with five flats in each floor. That was when Kayole was still infested with muggers and getting tenants was a nightmare. But he thought that was modest, and was away from scrutiny. Ostentation brought problems.

The excitement at the announcement of marriage banns with Hazel camouflaged his new found wealth (the car basically) and the congregations and the electoral college members, wanting to be on Bishop Silas' best books clamoured for his future son in laws accession to the seat of Bishop.

New parishes in Naivasha were introduced and after whirlwind election, wedding and honeymoon in Zanzibar, Cornelius and Hazel came back for enthronement. The case of the priest was attracting attention still, and there was speculation about another mysterious black priest of unknown name and abode or church that had arrived at the scene and gave the phone number of the mission. One police man had noted the phone number of the car, and the car had been found in Mombasa having been used in a robbery. The driver who had no identity on him was a look alike of

Cornelius, but was shot dead during the robbery. MacDonald only told him not to worry as the unit was in the country working things out.

Before the enthronement, Cornelius engineered the creation of a post, Bishop emeritus and asked that Bishop Silas hold that post. His enthronement was one of the largest gatherings, with visitors from his college and many different churches, ethnic communities and politicians from across the political divide. A new era for the Church of Pentecost in Kenya had begun.

STOP THIEF

Johnny Turner was not as white as his name implies. He was of a skin whose hue you could put at ebony and get away with the little scientific classification.

A hardworking man, he had already graduated with a B.Com degree from one of the campuses of our National University, first class honours. You'd be disappointed as I was when I learnt that he didn't take the next logical step. The Faculty of Commerce bombarded him with letters and reminders that the Masters Programme was about to start. But he had made his decision. Too much education would not fill his pockets and bring meaningful prestige. If your head was too full, it became clogged, and God knows the number of loonies strutting our campuses: unimaginative geniuses with solutions to every problem, an unswerving loyalty to empty loaded talk and predilection against practical application.

So sharp was he that by the time he was graduating, he had passed all the stages in accounting and was a recognized Certified Public Accountant. Life, for all intents and purposes, was smiling at him.

Working for a government dealing with issuing Import-Export trading licenses was not the kind of work he considered his cup of '*chai*'. But there he was, making 'the best out of a bad situation' as he often assured his sceptical friends. He had learnt in the hard school of accounting that absolute honesty was lunacy, and that honesty in itself is not a prized business commodity. In life, influence peddling was more important than raking off hard cash from your victims.

Influence peddling meant that you had to be a conscientious public servant, helpful to those in need and obliging even with what others considered trifles. A bent pen here, a crooked ledger there: business as usual. Never ask for bribes, in fact, never, never take bribes. Then people will be all too anxious to bring forth gifts. And human beings are a funny lot, Johnny Turner mused. They would bring their daughters and some would even bring their wives!

But he was a man of certain moral sensibilities, so he didn't accept them. Then some would hive for you acres off their farms, others shares in their companies, yet others would just give you part of the goods you helped them export or import.

Some daring ones even gave money, discretely. He accepted them. Like this car he was now driving. An Opel Astra KAD. Part of a consignment of 100 he helped import at reduced duty payment. One had been driven up to his gate, the log-book and the key presented to him.

The traffic was atrociously slow this morning. Especially on Jogoo Road. He was beginning to crawl with little money earners who bought second hand cars, or Nissan Sunny rec's and drove them in a not too gentlemanly manner. This irritated him. And somebody with an old 404 had dared scratch his fender! The case was with the insurance investigators and they'd be only too glad to pay the figure demanded by Johnny since they knew on which side their bread buttered.

Elegance and charm are the stocks of the trade, thought Johnny, joining Haile Sellaise Avenue. You had always to be smart to mean business. On the other hand, charm often assured your clients of your culture, refinement, and put them in appreciative mood for the little help they got. A crazy driver going towards City Square shot ahead of him from the first lane, almost ripping off the nose of his car as he took the roundabout to join Moi Avenue. 'Damn' he swore aloud and nosed his car perfectly forward in the second lane. He always parked at the basement of KENCOM house although he worked at the Ministry of Finance, along Harambee Avenue.

This was a habit he had developed when he discovered that Noela followed the route from City Square Post Office to Standard Chattered, Moi Avenue, where she worked as the secretary to the manager of the Foreign Exchange Section. He would saunter lazily round past the American Embassy, Ex-Telecoms, Central Bank, and round again to the Finance Ministry Building. He never failed to meet Noela along the route each morning, especially as she had to pick mail each morning before going to work. If his love for Noela was the gin for his ardour, then their morning encounters were the tonic which helped the gin push him throughout the day before their coffee encounters. Sometimes they ended up on the same bed, needless to say.

As he parked his car this morning, he had very pleasant thoughts. He had discovered last week that it was Noela birthday he didn't know which year, but he suspected she could range from 22-24 years old, give or take one year. He counted himself some kind of an expert in female agrology. This was any woman's secret weapon. So this Friday, he had set a meeting and was sure he would give her a nice surprise – a gold engagement ring and a diamond necklace.

Ramesh would bring the presents, of course. He had helped sanction a deal involving several million dollars with the Central Bank for this particular trader. Ramesh had been anxious to give him some money but he had flatly refused.
'Take it my fwend.You have served werywerywell. This no bribe money. Just take buy your wife present.'
'No Ramesh. You are such a good friend. I wouldn't imagine taking money from you. I am not even married, yet.
'When you *vant* (want) marry?'
'I don't know yet. I think I ought to give her an engagement ring next Friday. Your friend Rahul gave me a very nice necklace for her last month – gold'.
'Consider you'll get quality service this time. No joke'
'Oh. I didn't mean to…' Johnny started.
'No worry my '*fwend*' Ramesh cut in, 'Your wife be a good woman. I get you engagement rings and necklaces for her. *Ven*you*vant* this?'
'Friday would be just fine.'
'Rings – pure gold. Necklace be pure diamond. You fear no failure.'
'No failure between friends!' Johnny Turner chuckled, a gratified grim spreading on his face.
That deal had been sealed with little ado. He knew Ramesh well.

He dealt in gold and diamonds and had huge concessions from the government to monopolize the 'invaluable market' as trading in these two things was known. God knows where he mined his gold and diamonds. But he was certain of one thing: his present of gold rings and diamond necklace would be real.

He was glad he was not the one putting his signature on the licenses. He prepared data and gave his bosses to sign. They asked him a question or two and he gave them the answers Ramesh wanted him to give. The papers had been processed so quickly he thought there was a new baptism in the civil service. Then he realized there must be some grease oiling the joints of the officials.

Ten billion shillings is not an amount you disburse easily but Ramesh got paid. His scheme, he said, was earning the country a lot in foreign currency. But there, Johnny's knowledge ended. He decided to take a backseat and strictly no cash. Gold and Diamonds never lose their value, but money dances in the stock market exchange. And the income tax would move in fast when money swelled in an account. That would mean bribing of officials concerned and he didn't like the thought of bribing others to save himself. No, with Ramesh and Rahul, it must be gold or diamond upfront. He looked up as he emerged from KENCOM basement and saw his Madonna about to start crossing the car park between Tumaini House and KENCOM.

His Madona, Noela, was a girl with something to show. She was a girl that answered to the name girl. She was not a woman, she was not a girl. She was simply a girl, and to Johnny Turner, she was the girl. They had met at a banker's party where he had gone to represent his boss, the permanent secretary in the Finance Ministry.

Now as Noela walked in that peculiarly provocative way of hers, she thought of Johnny Turner and a languid smile creased her face. When he had been introduced to give a speech on behalf of the permanent secretary, she had expected a white man to climb to the podium. The tall handsome man with distinguished air that had risen had literally turned her on. Now what she waited for was the opportunity to turn on Johnny Turner.

And Turner was turned on that very night.

After his speech, Turner had seen her striking beauty and immediately come over. He was caressing a glass of wine which he sipped from every now and again.

'Do I know you?' Turner asked.

'That's a loaded question.' She had calmly replied.

'Sorry if I sounded rude. Are we acquitted?'

'Yes. I have seen you speak and observed you for some time.' Obviously, you've also been observing me. So here we are acquitted.'

He was disconcerted with her every minute. He knew a direct attack might work here better than gentlemanly tackling. Nevertheless, he thought he'd try once more.

'The evening is quite pleasant. You pressed for time?'

'Definitely not. Hoping for a date?'

'As a matter of fact I am.'

'That will depend on whether I am convinced I am a lamb consorting with another lamb.'

'For starters. We could slip away and start talking seriously. But I must warn you I won't manage the guise of a lamb very long.'

'Since I am reassured for the present, why don't you assure me also of my means home?'

'You married?'

'I had not met prince charming before'. She challenged.

'I see.' he lamely replied. 'Give me a minute to go round some guests, then I will be right back. My Astra is at the parking, waiting for a precious gem to take home,' with that, he steered himself around the room with elegance, oozing charm and masculinity.

She followed his every movement with her eyes. In his wake, women turned to stare. A few were looking enviously in her direction, she noted with satisfaction. After some ten minutes, she came back.

'Ready to be sacrificed?' he asked.

'This is not the place not the time', she retorted.

They were out and the attendant saluted them as they entered his car.

'Will I be told the name of my beautiful female escort?'
'Noela.'
'The first direct answer. I might be breaking through the ice finally.'
'It doesn't complement your efforts really. It is pure sympathy. I happen to have philanthropic feeling this night.'
'And where does the lady philanthropist work?'
'Why?' asked Noela.
'Hanging out with that banker's crowd'…
'I am not a banker.' She interrupted.
'…means you work in the establishment'.
'I am the secretary to the Forex manager, Transtrade Bank, Stan chart Towers.'
'Oh. And to think this prince charming has snatched his lass from under his nose!' He showed absolute sorrow.
'You don't sound worried. As for the charming bit, I am yet to make up my mind.'
'Then what about magnetic?'
'Sticky would be fairer judgment. Something to do with glue.' He stopped the car in front of a Chinese restaurant and led her in. He introduced himself and they were led to the table he had booked. The dim candle light in the corner table created a romantic atmosphere. The waiter, a short china man of indeterminate age withdrew after supplying their wants. Johnny Turner briefly wondered why a Chinese would come thousands of mile away from home to set up a restaurant. The bill put paid to such doubts.

'You are such an avid eater. I thought you'd open your plea during super.' Noela declared.
'I have changed my mind.'
'And why, if I may ask?'
'Because you've taken my breath away.'
'Interesting.' Observed Noela.
The table was cleared and coffee brought.
'You are looking at me so hard your eyes might pop off your head.'
'Is it? It is a bad habit I picked up in the Hotel when I laid my eyes on you.' Johnny said.
Pause.

'I have never learnt how to tell a girl I love her.'

'Now have you not?'

'But today for once, I can tell you that without batting an eyelid.' Johnny said, as if his train of thought was continuing.

'I take that as a wink.'

'There is a say that the spirit is willing but the body is weak. Do you think it is the truth?'

'What are you suggesting?'

'That I drive you home when the spirit for such a stupid thing is strong.'

'Good idea. I wasn't hoping for more'

With these, they left the restaurant and entered the car.

Johnny turned on his quarry after putting the key in the ignition. He found the lips waiting, full, warm and luscious.

After a few moments, she pulled away panting. Johnny Turner was heavily breathing. It was moments before any of them spoke. For Turner, it was the revelation of the kingdom itself. He swore to be true to his gem. Noela, on the other hand, felt the security and dependability that Johnny exuded. A state of bliss hung on the air around them. It was a halo that twined their paths and fates irrevocably on that day. True, they were not innocent of the ways of the world. But this was something inchoate.

Johnny had driven her home that night. He discovered that she resided in Denholm, not a very great distance from Buru-Buru. Their affair had blossomed progressively that now marriage hung in the air like a tantalizing fruit. She felt she could not deny that to her Johnny. And with that instinct unique to some women, she knew the proposal was soon coming. And moreover she would not stall him.

Joe Mondo, 'the ripper' as he was known in the shadowy world earned his name the same way he earned his living: ripping; off expensive necklaces, wristwatches, bangles and such other paraphernalia from the rich. Most of his victims were ladies unaccompanied and sometimes a few men got a taste of his medicine. It was not uncommon for him to rip a resisting 'client' with a knife as he put it, 'for their own good'.

Even in his world, he was considered an 'elite toughie', for he knew how to cover his flanks – he said his 'arse'. This elicited a lot of envy from other 'le Emperors' who ruled other operational districts in which they divided Nairobi. Joe Mondo went to school, passed highly and joined the University. He fell victim to an axe wielding vice-chancellor who saw him as a threat to public security after a verbal tiff over conditions at the campus. From that, he learnt to serve only himself and his god. And his god was money. So every morning he would wake at dawn, and dress to go and take offerings for his god. Sometimes he would be busy up to mid night.

In his 'business', you had to dress well to survive. He learnt that, being a business man', appearances are very important. It did not serve for one to be taken for a thug. There were many hazards to poorly dressed people.

The police could take one for a criminal and the blood thirsty public was even worse.

He dreamt of the day when he would retire honourably, raise a family and count his blessings. Today he turned out in a blue pin-striped suit, a white shirt and a matching flowered tie. He had visited his hairdresser yesterday. He checked his Seiko wristwatch and knew that the job he had planned for some weeks was about to be executed. It may add a quarter of a million to his pension scheme which by the last reckoning had hit 2.5 million. It was 7.30 am and he had 15 minutes take or add two to execute the manoeuvre. He strolled to the porch of Green Corner Restaurant where he picked the day's paper and times magazine. He looked at his shoes and his image smiled back at him. Satisfied, he sauntered to the front of Kenya Commercial Bank and waited.

Nothing new. The shilling was still at its gymnastics. The World Bank and the club du Paris was still wrangling with the government over new aid. The political scene was theatre of the absurd. The ruling party was still basking in its victory at the polls dubbed free and fair by the western powers. The so called opposition was wrangling over the person to be the official leader of opposition in parliament. The defection of two of their members hung in the air like the sword of Damocles. 'Shit' it was good he was apolitical.

Three minutes to the time. He could see the man walking from the KENCOM parking. His gaze shifted down the pavement on the side of Moi Avenue, towards the American Embassy. He saw her coming. It was all a glitter on her throat. 'Whew! How easy it would be to remove it! And how sweet it would feel in the pocket! Two minutes. He started walking in concert with the man.

The dreamy stupid smile was on his face. How he hated those who worshipped love! Especially if the man was a boot licking college mate who never complained about it when his peers were complaining. It was his likes that made Mondo get expelled. Love was a transient, predatory phenomenon. One minute. The man had seen her. She did not see the man. They were almost on one another and in that instant SWISH! And the gold necklace was gone. Johnny Turner saw something that dazzled his eyes. He did not know what had hit her. But he saw in a split second that the god necklace was gone. Noela was in hysterics. She had fallen down and was clutching her hand bag and shrieking thief! Thief! As she pointed hazily at Johnny who loomed over her helplessly. She shouted even harder for help.

In a minute, there was bedlam all over. Blows started landing on Johnny Turner from all quarters. He laughed at the apparent joke and this enraged the mob even more. As more stones landed on him, he heard one person rail at 'these well-dressed conmen and robbers'. It was then that it dawned on him why they were beating him. He tried to shout his innocence and declare his love for Noela for but no sound came from his mouth. A long way off, he saw Noela, an angel dressed in white and wreathed in gold and diamonds beckoning to his and wondered whether he would reach her. A gulf separated them. Something heavy landed on his head and took a gigantic step and landed next to Noela. But she was gone and he grasped at thin air.

The crowd had produced gasoline and matches. Motorists had stopped their vehicles on Moi Avenue and along the access. They came out for the spectacle, thirsting for blood. It was one of them that produced the gasoline. Everyone complained about the spate of thefts and violent robberies and each wanted to be the one to light the match. Finally, it was decided to hold an impromptu election for the two posts. One person to pour the gasoline and the other to light the match.

Meanwhile, 'the ripper' had reached the top floor of Diamond Trust Towers and was looking down at the scene. He saw that it was turning nasty. There was a traffic jam all over the town as far as the eye could see. Motorists were leaving their vehicles and coming to investigate what was the matter. It resulted in further confusion and the whole of Nairobi congealed into one huge traffic snarl-up. Some police on the beat stood complacently by. But a team of Anti-riot squad arrived at the scene and mingled with the crowd. They lost contact with each other and were robbed of their walkie-talkies. Some of the crowd could be seen wielding the police shields and truncheons with abandon. It was useless throwing their tear gas canisters into the crowd.

Near the mangled body of Johnny Turner, the 'election' was being decided on a crooked *'mlolongo'* form. It was the most effective form to elect the executioners. Two smartly dressed men were elected and they proceeded methodically to their task. Soon, black chocking smoke billowed from the body and this demarcated the epicentre of the conflagration. Johnny Turners last sensations were of intense heat and it translated into a burning thirst. He licked his lips. How he felt like a drop of water to slake his thirst. Ouch! The agony of it all! He too looked at the billowing smoke and felt it had something to do with his thirst.

A police helicopter started to circle overhead. Their loud speakers blared to restore order. Motorists were advised on the routes to take. Motorists who lost their vehicles were told to check for them either at Uhuru Park or the City Stadium. Those who failed to get their vehicles were to report to the Central Police Station. But the traffic would not budge long after the smoke had died. Noela was being lifted into an ambulance. It sped on pavements towards the American Embassy, HaileSellaise Avenue, and towards Kenyatta National Hospital. Her hysterics had resulted into a comma. Doctors gave her a gloomy chance.

Joe Mondo had an overwhelming sense of defeat. He had not planned it this way. A dead client was unproductive. And though this was his 'district', the other operators would feel the heat of police and public indignation for a time to come. And then he would have to change territory. He was too prestigious to go beyond Tom Mboya Street. But the operators of the 'Fire Station – Ebrahim', 'Kimathi', 'ICEA', 'Lillian Towers' and 'Nyati House' Districts were averse to any switches of territory. They would gladly gobble him up or promote one of their lackeys to his place. He had to work out a deal with the weakest before they fell on him like wolves. They've often faulted him for being 'too smart' and he had to use his repute to survive in this jungle. He would be calling on 'King Knife Edge', the 'Emperor of Nyati District at midnight today.
The rest he left to God. He hopped it would soon be business as usual.

THE LOVE THAT LUSTS

Mary – May-Ree was a beautiful girl. Let us start with her name that I confess I always find romantic Sounding.

When she was born, her parents were not as sophisticated as they are today. We must admit though, that, judging by the standards of these days, the parents were the bright spots of black dark pre-independent African Countryside.

Her father, after finishing primary 8, was acknowledged as a man of knowledge and given the task of making sure that the village school imparted Knowledge to the ignorant African boys (you will excuse me if I talk of boys mostly, because those days' girls were not expected to go to school. More often, those girls who went to school would snap the chain of traditional restraint and sin with spirits. They would then be called 'Ochodo-ororo' in the Luo language. This has been shortened to 'ochot' which expresses the full force and vulgarity of the English equivalent – prostitute. And I say sin with 'spirits' since a woman cannot prostitute on herself without help from a man. In Africa, I haven't yet heard of the idea of a male prostitute talked about, so it really must be that the educated African girl in these days would sin with spirits.

And now, about the beautiful girls name. But first let me explain to you the position of the father, and how come he called the girl by that romantic and throaty name that makes my spirit of adventure rise.

Miss Jeanette Jones was working with the Phelps Stokes, when the foundation was trying to spread the idea that African brains, because they were too big, had not the refinement for concepts except to co-ordinate their reflexes and muscles. And in order to exploit this human potential for the development of the human race, the African educational priority had to change from concept orientation to technical adaptation to their environment.

May-Rees father had just been promoted to the job of a head-teacher and after reading an American educational journal about support for schools oriented towards technical education, had written to their liaison office in East and Central Africa based in Kenya requesting for a visit to his school to assess possible areas of co-operation or assistance.

Miss Jeannette Johns Land Rover was not a most reliable gift from God through the British colonial government officials who seemed to have a bias against the 'Yankee Woman'. They gave her a car that would not keep schedules and she had to stop for long periods in the jungle enroute for the engine to cool, before gingerly continuing her journey. Luckily, she knew the missions along the way and the missionaries always welcomed her and provided basic needs and one of them, father O'Leary, even repaired the car. So it happened that she arrived on Sunday, the eighth day after the birth of his beautiful pearl my pen is out to eulogise, when the local catechist was about to conduct the baby's baptism.

And so the process of name choosing had to be halted as this lady with power from the land across the seas brought her faulty Land Rover to a sighing exhausted rest. It coughed, spluttered, shook but finally breathed deeply and sucked off the motor. In the class, which also acted as a church, the process of name choosing had been painfully slow. The Bible is hard to interpret, especially when you need to distinguish evil names from saintly ones that befit such a beautiful girl as the one born to the head teacher. So they had been arguing whether Esther was right in choosing to stay back and dine from the table of abundance while her people suffered from the hands of the same monster she dined with.

When this illustrious lady from the land smiled and asked to be given the child to hold. She carried the child in wonderment and declared: She's so beautiful that only one image fills my mind: that of the mother of Jesus; May-Ree! Quickly the catechist had declared the two names of saints good and baptized the teachers daughter May- Ree. And so her name had remained to this day. But that had been long ago, and we can't remember clearly because 30 years is not yesterday.

May-Rees mouth was beautiful as her name. The lips were luscious like a fruit full of wet sap, and shaped as if perpetually saying May-Ree. She was chocolate brown and no part of her head had a mischance with the chisel.

The head rested on a breath taking neck that was not too longhand was rounded by three natural beauty lines like priceless beadsman artists own. Her body was well formed, with the buttocks complaining slightly of the size of even the free-est. dress worn and the breasts sharp sticking like two lump posts, heads of mushrooms when they break the ground for the suns world. When she walked the breasts would shake slightly like two proud dancers, aware that their dance was as captivating as it was tantalizing. The hips, too, had their share of making the picture. They were so well formed and full, and, considering the length of the legs on which they 'Sprouted' from, they gave much promise. Her knees always made me swallow Saliva, and do worse, especially when I dreamt of their parting. A normal occurrence really since we grew up together.

Much and enough for her beauty. When May-Ree was 18, her suitors could be forestalled no more. She had to choose a lover anyway. And she was not a girl who would snap the chains of societal restraint, despite the fact that she was to join the university after her form six. And for a woman of her education too, it was surprisingly she accepted to be married before 'finishing' her education.

The first suitor was a handsome, masculine man of 25 who was an Architect by profession. He had come to know the family of May –Ree when only 22 after graduating from the university. The father, now a senior figure in the government of Kenya, had wanted to construct a family residence, which would also be a flagship of his success. The young man had introduced himself and his profession and the old and young man warmed up towards one another. The same evening, May-Rees father had invited Adonis Omano to his house to discuss his project. They agreed and the young man produced a design at a much reduced cost and beauty and magnificence that took his breath away and made him soar on wings.

79

The construction was done with the minutest supervision by the architect himself. It was during this time that sometimes the man (or boy, as he really was considered by the older man) would notice some shy looking beautiful girl, especially when he spent in their house. He used to find it funny that he would notice this girl, and sometimes catch himself gazing absentmindedly at night, visualizing the bliss of married –life with her.

After three weeks, he realized that he was losing his concentration and 'vision'; For Adonis Omano considered himself a professional and he believed in 'success first, life later' theory. So to make his life less unbearable, he collected his savings and bought a Toyota Crown, 2400cc, which would take him back to his house no matter what time he finished work at May-Ree father's residence.

Sometimes driving home through the forest that surrounded May-Ree fathers estate, he would find himself identifying with the older man, remembering of how rough life had been on him, and how, through grit, deviousness and determination, the old man posted such admirable success: he wanted to surpass that of the older man hundred fold.

He dreamt of buying an island in Lake Victoria and developing his family estate there. Sometimes he would stop his car, walk to the trees by the road and hug them fondly, whispering to them that he's going to make an even better, kinder home to their offspring. One day, the older man was to discover him in this state, talking to a flower in a trance. The older man advised him that younger men should not meditate but work and plan for their success.

Late in his 24th year, the young Adonis had realized the full potential of love and he could no longer deny vent to his feelings. With his business and experience rising, he felt more sure footed in life, and, one day as he sat in the older man's 3 storey success story, taking tea with his charming daughter, he felt a weightlessness seize him from his base and rise exhilaratingly to his head. His head felt lighter and as May –Ree bent to pour him more tea, he gently caught her arm, took the Kettle away and put it on the table firmly, then turned and fiercely kissed May-Ree. May-Ree responded mother like and held him for a full five minutes- an eternity-before she sat down shyly. Then in a bubble, he confessed his love and intention to May –Ree and the latter acquiesced, revealing the soft petals of love that filled her heart.

The relationship strengthened and in his 25th year, Adonis agreed with May-Ree that the only way to keep them from compromising with one another and shaming her parents was to propose a marriage to her parents. When they did this, May-Ree's mother was mildly surprised but declared that it was not out of the ordinary. She only thought May-Ree still wanted to 'finish' school and be a bit older.
I can only describe the demeanour of the father. The older man experienced exhilaration, pride and perplexity which were stifled by a non-committal grunt from what seemed his inner soul. He however signalled his agreement with the process and marriage plans were well underway.

On the eve of the wedding, which was also the last day of the 25th year of Adonis Omanos life, May-Ree's father organised for his daughter and son-in -law a farewell party. He invited many guests that included ministers, other luminaries and even got a congratulatory phone call from the president himself. The cocktail in his family home ended at 9 pm in view of the next day's heavy schedule. The guests left but Adonis lingered on, now generally accepted as one of the family. The older man felt a tear (of separation) rise in his eye and they went to sleep leaving the young people to take their time.

That night, he slept fitfully for he kept reminding himself to wait for the sound of Adonis car go away into the darkness. At about 12 pm, he fell into deep nightmarish sleep in which he fought and strangled a boy of his age who wanted to take away his wife from him. His wife, in his dream had the head of his wife but the torso and limbs of his daughter. When he woke up the next morning he was dishevelled distraught and anxious. He felt his feet soiled and saw his night gown almost torn. He then woke his wife and asked her to ring Adonis to confirm that he wassafe and sound.

The phone kept ringing without an answer. The older man took a bath and then went to wake up his daughter whom he found sleeping deeply, having not changed from last night's sleep. He asked her when Adonis had left and she said at about 12 pm. He urged her to prepare, declaring with some humour that his cherub must sign in the day of the loss.

At exactly 9 am, they were ready waiting for the May-Ree's maids to arrive. The church was 15 minute drive and the service would start a 9.30am.

At 9.15 am, when they were getting impatient, a car entered their gates flying and skidded to a screechy stop in front of their door. Within the space of suspended time, the man had burst in and blurted the word dead. The older man went to a state of shock and begun kicking in painful paroxysms. An ambulance was immediately summoned. May-Ree just said calmly: 'I know Adonis Omano is dead. Please leave me alone.'

And so I rest my pen on that score. But I must tell you, my friend one more bit of information: Adonis Omano was found strangled with a belt about 100 metres from his car which was left with, the motor running, lights on and with an open door. There seems to have been no struggle, and he died smiling.
So Adonis Omano died and his case rested. When May-Ree was 29 years old, she attended a conference on the 'Question of Women and Classical Attitudes'. This conference was done in New York, and all leading female personalities attended it. Prime Ministers, politicians, scientists, social workers, doctors, teachers etc. all graced the conference. The drift of the conference was the empowerment of women for leadership. Time had passed since Adonis Omano's death.

That night, she had met and fell in love with a lonely but powerful leader of the Negro Uprising in the Muslim brotherhood. She insisted that, they could not 'go all the way' before he met his father and hears the old man's view.

At first Louis Jenkinson was reluctant. For one, he did not want to go and sleep in a cave or to meet with a race that walked naked in equatorial heat. His mind was filled with Lions, Cheetahs, Panthers, Leopards, hyenas and wild pigs in animistic dances' to the eerie tom toms of the African night. No. After finding his jewel he did not want to plunge in the shame of her origin. It was good to sleep in a New York hotel alone than to sleep with an angel amid sheep bleating all the time. This, however, he did not share with his love. How could you tell one whom you love and cherish that you do not like her background?

In the end, his curiosity and sense of adventure drew him out and as soon as the conference was over, they flew back to Kenya on a British Airways Flight. On arrival, the father who had been notified by telex had sent a chauffeured car which took them to the family estate to an expense –does – not matter welcome.

After Louis Jenkinson had bathed, shaved and rested, the father took him on a tour of his magnificent estate in an open jeep.

The 'Negro' leader was greatly surprised, at this man's appreciation of beauty that spoke the poignancy of his inner soul. They passed the flowers, the trees, the vegetable gardens, the fruit sections and the monkeys that roamed the estate! Then they went to his ranch and saw his Friesian, deep into an expanse of land hidden with coffee trees. Jenkinson believed, fell in love and was converted. If a black man, whom the white race in the US had taught them was useless could build the airport he saw and plan his estate with such aesthetic finesse, why, the colored folks back home must be proud of their heritage. For Louis Jenkinson saw no dancing savages and slept not in a cow pen.

At night, the family ate and then conversed lazily until the subject was broached. The older man expressed his hope that the marriage would last, saying that he knew the American Society to be marked by divorce. 'To you' he said, making a philosophical posture, 'marriage is incomplete without a divorce.' But the young man insisted on the purity of his feelings and the matter rested at that. It was agreed that the Young man would go back to New York the morrow day and return for a wedding in a week's time. When the father looked at May-Ree and saw her happiness, he felt downcast. Then she caught his eye and for a fleeting moment recognised an aggressive defiance in the man. Something in that look made her heart give a wild beat of fear and a lurching of premonition.

When she went to sleep, she slept soundly but in a nightmare, she saw a traditional god-like figure of a man she vaguely recognized plunge a Knife on the heart of her lover.
Her father woke up feeling tired. He was so tired that he thought he had been wrestling the whole night. When he went to check on his guest, Louis Jenkinson's lay dead on his bed. His face was a perplexed frown.

When the death was reported to inspector Valerie Motomo, she went with her team and viewed the scene. She decided that there was not much struggle, except a slight twitch in the man that might have been the convulsion of death.
She then contacted the Commissioner of police, who contacted the Foreign minister. The Foreign minister personally conveyed the message to the American Ambassador who sent a representative, specialists were sent from Washington to perform the post-Mortem examination and they drew a blank. Seemingly, there was no sign of diseased tissue, nor was there sign of struggle.

They started advancing theories. The police pathologist suggested that there was possibility of death due to intense heat or prolonged stay in the sun during the tour of the Estate in an open jeep. But the American specialist said noway. The brain should not be opened at all costs since that would be an exercise in butchery. And so Louis Jenkinson, and the secrets of his death with it.

But Inspector Valarie Motomo was not satisfied. She called May Ree aside and asked her what had brought the American to their house. She explained the nature of their relationship and their plans. At one point, Inspector Motomo felt that she was getting paranoid and was jumping to conclusions. For one thing, she felt extremely jealous of May-Ree, for the attention of every man was drawn to her even when she just turned her head.

Then she asked on whether the father had given then consent to marry and she replied in the affirmative. Did she notice something else? Yes, the father seemed to be accepting the marriage as some unkind fate. She thought he feared his daughter's fiancée might die again.
Had your fiancé died earlier? Pressed inspector Motomo. Yes. Under what circumstances? On the eve of our wedding. How did he die? He was strangled. Was the culprit found? No. what item did you find at the scene? Only his car and an old belt of fathers. How long ago? Nearly four years.
She kept quiet, puzzled. She wanted to ask some more but knew how far one went into the family's affairs without arousing suspicion or hurting feelings. She wanted to ask May-Ree, for example, her relationship with her dad.

A month from the time of Jenkinson's death, Inspector Motomo invited May-Ree to visit her. Valerie's husband was working as a psychiatrist and had a very successful clinic. He introduced them, and she could see that the husband was fascinated by May-Ree's beauty, even intimidated by her presence.

When May-Ree was taking a bath, Valerie asked her husband what he thought of her. Her husband admitted that he felt 'captured', and had a slave-like feeling. Would you feel like that if you were the father? Yes. What would be your reaction? At least consciously? I would be very jealous of any man trying to love her, because that man would be a rival to me for her affection. I would feel a murderous rage which can present itself in two ways: one, I would be outwardly hostile to any man who proposes marriage and would give every excuse why my daughter has not found an appropriate suitor, second, I might be outwardly happy but subconsciously wish to murder the man. And should an opportunity present itself, even in my sleep, I would murder him.This situation would happen even in a dream. If in a dream I dreamed that I have murdered the man, it might as well be true if I were a dream walker. However people talk of the spirit or the shadow killing, or acting in certain ways on behalf of the physical.

"It is a common phenomenon in Africa of wizards often to be active only in their shadow-spirit form. This happens when the person, who is by birth a wizard, or whom spirits of the dead demand of to be a wizard, has the will to command him physically against the practice.

'Therefore at night, his soul develops another form and commands him to do actions of a wizard. It would therefore be a long shot, indeed quite disputable, that the soul of May-Ree's father might be working in such a manner. Moreover with these instances, it is normally disputable whether it is not the soul of the perceiver that wills for him a physical form of one who is innocent to perceive doing such evil acts. Some dispute this and say that when you beat this form, the actual body of this man is likewise injured. But so also would it happen were one with a strong willed evil soul wish ill on one. He would then wrought injury on the body of the one he has directed his wrath.

Mr Motomo paused, regarding his wife as the latter followed his argument, spell bound. Then he concluded.
'This Scenario is rare in history, and psychologists do not take it seriously. But we could investigate it in May-Ree's father if we can make favourable situation that is his jealousy must be aroused, with May-Ree participating fully,"
'Yes I will, piped May-Ree strangely calm. Inspector Valarie Motomo caught her breath sharply and gurgled the words she was about to say while her husband released a strangled groan of helplessness.

'Don't fret. I listened to your narrative and got carried away. It was quite convincing, because often I have had a feeling that I'll never get married so long as my father is around. I've often felt he was in some way connected to these deaths but I have had no evidence to go on. It has made me superstitious thinking that because he wishes me ill-luck inwardly these misfortunes have to occur.'

Valarie recovered and said: Will you act as my husband's lover? And even flaunt him to your parents?

'Yes, so long as he does not compromise me, really'

'Then what Mr. Motomo will do is to start visiting you and act fond. Sometimes go with him to yourroom and act lover like. Your father will be curious. If he asks, tell him the truth, rather lie, that you are lovers and you do intend to be his concubine. Then Mr. Motomo will take on from there.

They talked on late into the night and after thrashing on all the details went into wakeful slumber. There was a rapport between the three of them. A sense of experiment, of scientists in a laboratory with a rat in Skinners Box enveloping them.

'When May-Ree's father saw Mr Motomo, he was filled with a sense of dread but then he overcame this and became very pompously courteous. Mr Motomo, the psychologist was a perfect lover actor. After three weeks, May-Ree's father patience was worn out. He had been trying to wait for May-Ree to declare to him that this was a lover. He was furious, reasoning that a young girl had no business messing around with a married man. He felt a premonition of the unknown.

Then one day, a knife had seared his heart. He had asked May-Ree about their relationship and she answered simply 'concubine'

'Concubine!' bellowed May-Rees father, almost bringing down the ceiling.

'Yes' Valarie said. 'Since my lovers whom I want to marry turn out dead on the wedding day, I might as well circumvent that'

'You are mad', he said in a strangled voice, his breath coming in short quick gasps.

'Time I was, declared May-Ree, in mock annoyance. May-Ree's father had not trusted himself and had gone to his study clutching his chest.

All the going on had been reported to Valarie Motomo. Her husband was a fine editor of the happenings; especially of the real longing absentminded looks he had occasionally caught himself giving May-Ree. But he was a real scientist and a sense of duty bound him to act well.

Then Valarie decided to move in. First Mr Motomo had to sleep in the house. Valarie and a team of policemen would me in the vicinity and at the sign of danger; an alarm would be activated to inform them to move in.

87

This would be through some doors May-Ree would leave open for them to use. They would then catch her father or his spirit in the act and punish him accordingly.

Since now the old man had his own bedroom, Inspector Valarie herself hid in one of the wardrobes and waited. May-Ree and Motomo went to 'sleep' after a high profile 'party' during which music had blared and ripped through the first floor where May-Ree rooms were. They retired with soft music, and soon, there was none at all and the lights went off.

From her observatory in the wardrobe where she was sufficiently suffocating, Inspector Motomo observed the old man dejectedly slip into pyjamas and drop into bed. But he hardly slept, for no sooner had he put off the light than he started twitching. Threatened with suffocation, and unable to see, Inspector Motomo opened the door and found May-Ree's father contorted torso twisted in pugilistic agony. His body was convulsing and his mouth foaming. This made Valarie to think of a doctor and she swiftly rushed downstairs and called for a flying doctor service. In her confusion, she had forgotten to observe what the man was doing. She remembered her duty and rushed back to find the older man's hands around a bed post as if he was strangling it.

Strangling! My husband's life is in danger! And with that thought she rushed to the room. May-Ree was sleeping on while Mr Motomo's hands flailed weakly against the air. In a split second, Valarie had woken up a fazed May-Ree and asked her to hold Motomo protectively and stop him from fighting. Then Valarie rushed to the old man's bedroom and wrestled with the man to release his hands strangling the bed post. When it became clear that she was fighting a losing battle, she decided to strangle the old man herself.

She felt the old man respond instantly by jerking his head up, but still, he was sleeping. As she squeezed harder and harder, the man's grip on the bedpost slackened. Then the old man's limbs hung limp and he breathed normally and begun to snore. When Valerie went to check on her husband he was so mighty shaken and narrated to them how someone had held his

88

neck in a vice like grip and he felt he was dying. Then suddenly they were released. As the copter of the Flying Doctors took off with May-Rees dazed father and the stunned Mr. Motomo, Valarie remarked to May-Ree that there was no sustainable case against her father and that he wouldbe sent for psychiatric treatment.

May-Ree woke up her mother and informed her that the father had had some kind of attack and was taken to hospital. She also told the mother that she was going on a long journey and would be back some day, not to worry. It is ten years since she left.

USUAL DELIGENCE

Let not a false impression be created in your mind that it is only in the teaching profession where we have lazy louts, practiced loud mouths and quislings who, well aware of their shot comings but not wanting to believe it, ingratiate, themselves with the head of the institution and then make it their business to mislead the head and generally survive in the confusion thus created.

It is the beginning of term three. Teaching is still slack. I had decided to put up a shack at my place and had to get time to go and shop for some materials this Friday afternoon. I had determined in my mind that I would not ask the Headmaster for an afternoon off. In my primary school, that time when students got taught from STUDENTS COMPANION, I learnt there is something called a French leave: not the leaves that make a French letter but a French leave.

Now how do you take a French leave? Obviously not by going to the HM and inventing a dead aunt you've just remembered her funeral. Nor do you plead illness because you might be required to give evidence after you've recovered. You don't go, of course to tell the HM the real reason, for your risk a reading of the Quran from him. The Quran is in the form of the Education Act which forbids him from giving teachers to go and do things that could be done at their free time as well as a leaf from the teaching ethics. In any case the first two tricks will be useful in the middle of the term when the fatigue that is teaching has caught up with you.

Now, you want to take a French leave. Being a conscientious teacher, obviously you don't leave your class doing nothing measureable. You call the class secretary and give him an assignment for the class which should be done in the first twenty minutes of the lesson, suffice it say theoretically. You tell him the work will be marked in class. From then on you are virtually free. But you hit the last nail of the plan. Appear very visible in the school. If the HM sneezes, go and check what the matter is. If there is a stray dog in the compound alert the HM to find the watchmen to remove it as a health hazard. That scheme of work you had taken to the secretary for typing at the end of the preceding term, make sure she does it today. When your presence has been considerably felt, pop off, just pop off, full stop. As the American say, period.

That afternoon however I had made it clear via a megaphone announcement that my afternoon lessons were on sale. I further declared that my vital interests were at crossroads with serving the Kenyan Child. I would take the fork which my vital interest followed. Mr. W was one among my audience who I could see captivated. He was head of my department; a position I somehow feel he knows he does not merit. I will not tell you that the guy is bankrupt of ideas, or that he lives on past glory that is ill defined. Let me explain why I felt Mr. W got excited by my public pronouncements. In the true form of a turncoat, Mr. W called my pronouncements insubordination and told me that if the 'computer' catches me off guard, then I have myself to blame. I countered that I will put a virus in the computer to obliterate all the information it contained, and that in any case, I am not a coward.

If it reached the day when the HM gets tired of me, why he would write a casualty to the Teacher Service Commission and like Joseph K, I will find a way to deal with my inquisitors. Mr. W then said: Mr. I, you've spoken like a man! You've shown you've got balls. Upon which I countered that I thought the woman in Beijing were speaking louder than me, and I had not gotten the opportunity in the short time to prove the potency of my balls- since I did not see any relevance in having balls that might not be working!

Tea was then brought to the staff room and teachers abandoned whatever they were doing and flocked around the table. Some were putting six spoons of sugar in the standard British cups. Though I take only one spoon of sugar in any tea-cup (no economic implication here) allow me to conjecture as to the whys of these teachers behaviour. You know many teachers cannot afford sugar in their houses. In the staff tea, a teacher has the opportunity to take all the sugar she/he needs in her/his system. So when she/he goes back to his house, he takes sugarless porridge and this is sweetened by the excess sugar he had taken in the staff tea. Mind, I haven't said that this teacher takes less than 4 cups. They are British you know, and the British have this habit of wishing to starve people. So the teacher has sugared his tea. Six teaspoonful's of sugar. Then enter the '*mandazi*' lady. You know, of course, that the teacher doesn't have money to pay in cash. He has to sweet talk the lady to continue extending his credit, citing the nearness of the end month. Madam, it is only twenty days to month end, surely you will get money! Finally he is given mandazi or a chapatti worth five shillings. She/he sits down for breakfast at 11 am.

So at 12.30 pm I went for lunch at my friends place. I have this arrangement with him since I stay far from school. At 1 pm, my friend told me to take him to his market stall on my way home. We go with him. At 2.30 pm, I decided to move on home, leaving my friend to settle accounts with his sales lady.

I start for home riding and whistling not for a particular reason but for lack of a better thing to do. I am sailing rather since it is sloppy. Then when I start to climb the hill, a familiar coat looms ahead, perched on a bicycle. I quickly catch up with him and you can imagine the shock on my face. It is the very W, 3 lessons that afternoon abandoned, going home. He tells me the HM told him he was going for some provisions in town, so the computer wasn't working. The HM boards a bus for Town and Mr. W. jumps on his bike. Beside, Mr. I, I don't have my child in that school. In any case my daughter is at home right now due to fee arrears. I don't see myself teaching anybody's child when my own daughter is not being taught!

There he rested his case. Anyway we had a nice ride to the town where I stay. He insisted I give him the marking scheme for our fourth form exams so we made a bee line for my house. I told him that other members of the department wanted to use it. He knew, of course. You don't become a Head of Department for no reason. He was going to be in school Monday noon since he had three lessons that afternoon. Not to worry, tell them. They'll get the scheme Monday noon.

Monday is one of my busiest days. I have three double lessons, the first one at 8.00 am. I thought without much to do and by the time I was finishing my fourth, time for tea and had arrived. Mr. W had not arrived. The other teachers ask me for the scheme and I tell them the HOD has it and he'll be here by noon. Two of my colleagues see no alternative but to reschedule their revision lessons. The other one is so sure Mr. W. will arrive in time since she will be teaching the lesson the same time as Mr. W will in another class. We could not help being optimistic about Mr. W's coming.

Coming from lunch, I find Miss J laying siege at my desk for the marking scheme. Mr. W. has not come back but she has to go and revise the exam with the students. Suppose we answered the questions and formed the marking scheme with the scraps I still remember? Fine, answers MissJ. She pulls out ten foolscaps, gives me a pen and flops down on a seat next to me, lays her charming head on my desk and goes to sleep. For a long moment my attention is riveted on a debate on whether to look at the rise and fall of breadth coursing through her body, trying to look towards the gate to see if Mr. W is coming, or answering the questions alone. Honour took hold of me and I flew through the questions, came up with a makeshift marking scheme and woke up Miss J. I explained to her the contours of the marking scheme and at the stroke of the bell, we were off to class for the last two lessons of the afternoon.

Tuesday 10 O'clock, Mr. W. makes an unobtrusive appearance. He is not having a loud mouth today. Nothing much happens. I notice though that the HM has put an alert for a staff meeting Wednesday. It was written in red indelible ink. I guessed that apart from the computer, the HM had also acquired infrared technology to aid him in administration of the school.

Wednesday come. Officially, the first lesson is to be taught before the meeting starts at 9 am. No teacher goes for it. The HM walks in to open the meeting at 11.30 a.m. with a lacklustre apology.
The first item of the agenda: Holiday tuition.
Don't be fooled. The HM starts with his usual lecture which takes fifteen minutes. By now, every teacher should be bored but they are not. They want to hear the direction of the HM's mind on this important matter. My

views had been clear. I had stated earlier for all to hear that setting the school term time table was a task better left for the curriculum developers.

Attempting to say that there should be extra teaching during the holidays is like saying that the Ladies and Gentlemen at the Ministry of Education including the Director of Education are daft and incompetent. But if that be your message, why don't you go and tell them this then occupy their offices? I also made it clear that this was like saying that the Kenyan child has a below average IQ, a view which I would disagree with. Or is it that the 8-4-4 education system is being derided at my expense? In all these cases, I found it wise to remain a teacher following the wise directives of the Ministry of Education.

The HM talks of teaching being a noble of profession. Fine. He says it is a call. I agree. But when he says our work should not be pegged to monetary emoluments, then I lose track of his speech. He drones on like an aero plane that passes you on a nappy afternoon.

I draw his picture mentally. This man doesn't even go to the local pub to break the elephants tusk. He does not even, like a good husband, accompany his wife to the market when she goes to buy provisions. When he leaves school, we breadth the a sigh of relief, not because he is a bad guy, but because we don't want him growing mouldy in this place then rubbing some of the mould on us who take the trouble to freshen ourselves. When he leaves school, he takes a bus from in front of the school to the provincial headquarters or to the capital city to buy what he needs in running the school. He sleeps at a relative's house or in a seedy hotel to keep expenses down. He comes back and alights at the gate with the goods he has brought. If you are hard up one day, don't approach this guy. He won't understand how a teacher reaches the bottom of the rock.

At one time I needed some money (the amount I will not disclose) and went to him. The guy looked at me, and perhaps because I'd never gone to him before, he felt compassion and told me to see the bursar. By the time I reached the latter's office, he'd already buzzed him to give me only $2/3$'s of what I'd requested. Upon which I told the bursar to keep his money since what I wanted the money for; I could not get for a lesser amount. Not wishing to extend the standoff, the bursar decided to give me the amount I had requested for. It is six months and I have only paid 1/3 of the money back.

The room had gone quiet. The HM had stopped talking and because he had presented the case, discussed it and concluded- naturally in favour of holding as tuition nobody is willing to say anything more or less. Then the HM looks around. People of my kind are quiet. But the HM's henchmen feel he's getting embarrassed. So three of them carry up their hands for the chairs notice. He chooses Mr. W, whom he feels is the most sensible among his minions. We smile at the compromise.

'Thank you for allowing me to express my views on the issue at hand. Sir, since the beginning of the year, we have been working so hard. Indeed the phenomena of missed classes is gone and the students are catching up well. What we need to keep the tempo up. In view of the marked improvement, and with all of us diligently attending to our duties as we have been doing, why can't we just scrap holiday tuition? The gap left will be filled with more lessons after four O'clock and Saturday mornings, which we will teach with our usual diligence'

A stifled giggle somewhere. I look at my friend. We have caught the attention of the other teachers. Silence, then more speeches. This time, the call to scrap the holiday tuition inundate the HM from the quarters he normally frowns upon. Momentum is too much and he's even assured that no teacher will attend the holiday tuitions unless the issue of emoluments is satisfactorily dealt with. You can imagine the sorrow etched on his face, then the resignation. Motion to abolish holiday tuition passed. My friend passes me a note. How many lessons did Mr. W. miss on Friday and Monday? I count on my fingers-six. Usual diligence indeed.

For me the meeting has ended. But we drone on until I am stirred by being named on a committee to prepare for some visitors who are to see us soon. I had planned to be away on that day. What will I do?

THE OFFICIAL DEATH OF A METEOR- CAPITALISED FOR CONSISTENCY

John Nalubowe was a man of substance. Not that he passed his primary seven with flying colours. He managed to go to Secondary School, yes, and when others were busy getting first division and second division and rushing to A-level schools, he landed a weak third and cooled his heels for one year, gaining experience at his father's shop.

In the next year, it took him three months to do some computer courses, which, of course, he passed highly. One day, while lazily reading a piece of one of the old daily papers he had purchased for wrapping purposes, he noticed an advertisement for a master's degree in Management and Business administration at the London School of Economics. Just as lazily, John Nalubowe decided to test his skills in official letter writing, applying to be registered for a master's degree in the school.

With alacrity that stunned rather than surprised him, he received a reply from the college advising him to join then in September of the same year. The only snag was that within six months of his programme, he had to sit for a higher diploma in the same, before he could proceed with his master's programme. Sit he did, and pass him passed.

Within two years, he had gained his higher Diploma and Masters in Management and Business Administration .Within the same year, he had a diploma in computer Programming.
He did not have to go far. As a brilliant Student, word had gone round about him and many firms offered him employment at various rates of remuneration. He wisely chose not to join established business. He went to a firm two years into business and within four months, he had risen to deputy directorship. He was so successfully that his director changed his position to that of Company Chairman and elevated him to an Executive Director. It was understood though, that he would have to go at some point, since his ambition may not be assuaged wholly by the company.

He hadn't cared that much, though, for he had been routing for just that. A man who knew that fame of personality had great value; he had started leaking his image into newspaper columns in Kenya.

In fact they called him a rising Business Executive, Computer Programming Specialist and wizard, A Successful Company Director etc. These accolades preceded his presence. Of course some of us didn't know who he was. We did not realize that this was the same boy we had walloped at exams in form four. In fact we never imagined that one of us could have obtained a master's degree and had had substantial experience in business and risen to such dizzying heights.

I wonder why the president did not give him a Head of States Commendation (HSC) or higher, something to do with a burning spear, for his rise and ambition was searing. .
Today, he drove his BMW, KAD something I can't remember (Because of the blood that he had later washed it), thinking and thinking hard.

And the worst thing, he had to meet a plague in the name of Susan for lunch. Susie, Susie, Susie. This is the girl that spurred mu attentions in form four. Falling in love with a Basketball player who had balls to match his brilliance in class, she had similarly dismissed him as a non-starter, Now four years later, just doing her second year at Campus with Pay As You Eat (PAYE) system, she thought better of her sentiments. Of course it was a matter of prestige, and since the star of her basketball lover had been dimmed by his failure to make campus (a really sad case since there was no reason except arrogant drunkenness that made him lose his rightful place), and the powerful shadow of John Nalubowe's star, nothing could prevent her changing allegiance. Of course it is like changing gear. When traffic light turns to amber, you shift the gear for the escape of traffic madness; it will be green soon.

A mad laughing of horns and cacophonous revving up of engines stunned him momentarily before he realized the light had turned to green. Quickly he engaged the gear and raced into Harambee avenue, then realised he had made a mistake, and doubled back to get to a Chinese restaurant not off

Koinange street and not far from the dreaded Nyati House. He parked the car and immediately his thoughts shifted to the business at hand, as he slowly walked to the lunch date.

It would be an enormous colossal loss for his company. The city inspectorate department had decided that the land on which they were constructing over 2,000 residential units was not for that purpose. That it was supposed to be a public rest area. Certainly the company could not bear a £ 1 billion loss.

Yet was it his responsibility? First, he had not been involved in the negotiation for the land. He had found that the land originally planned for low grade housing scheme had been left unused for twenty years. Yet the tax charged on it was rising and it was a striking distance from the city centre. He had looked around, drew a proposal and with his contacts, money for its development kept tumbling in. The Board at its annual meeting made it known that Mr Andrew Hayes, their American Director would need to renegotiate his engagement before the beginning of the next year.

John Nalubowe felt inkling that this deal was connected with Hayes imminent departure, somehow.
Blast! He fumed, entering the restaurant, to be led to the table he had reserved.

Susan, Suzy, Susie- whatever form she preferred, was already seated. She was dressed with striking elegance. Had he met her elsewhere, he could be forgiven for not recognizing her. Susan's hair was done to fall on her neck, undulating to her shoulders. Her face was ivory ashy brown, and on her nose dangled two shinny tiny rings, a sign of the glimmer within her breasts. Her mouth was painted deep red, giving her an air of constant expectancy, and heightening the glint of sex that surrounded her sleepy eyes. As for her neck, it was as elegant as ever, and even now, as she tossed her head delicately balanced on it, he felt an urge to take her and smash her with a ring of kisses to round it like an amorous necklace. An inchoate feeling that had not left him ever since he had desired her love and been spurred appeared. He was slightly stunned and touched by a rekindling of the old flame.

'Hi Dear!' she crooned from within her passionate, soothing throat rising to hug him as he reached the table. He was lost for words. He could only smile. As he helped her sit, he noticed two shiny full and luscious blobs peeping and protesting the imprisonment of her blouse. They rose gently, and just as gently fell with every soft breath of hers. In stupefaction, he dropped his spectacle case and begun fumbling for it on the ground.

The frowning waiter beat him to it and for a fraction of a second remained bent, looking at a carving of her lingerie that peeped promisingly from the high hem of her skirt. Inwardly he thought this is just a wide belt in the name of a skirt. When he came to, he observed the waiter going back bent as if a knife had been plunged in his bosom. A waitress was sent to relieve the stricken waiter, and John instantly knew what was amiss with the waiter, for he also felt an enormous rise of his manhood to painful proportions.

Sussie talked on unconcerned. All this had taken less than a minute. Presently his thoughts shifted to matters at hand.

1 billion pound loss! This would surely be an everlasting blot on his career. It had to be stopped at all costs. He smelt a powerful stench of collusion against him, somewhere. Well, let me talk to this inspectorate guy. Again he thought, going through the city development plans in his head, this was a mistake.

The waitress had put the food they somehow ordered and his attention was drawn to it.
He looked at Sussie who smiled unconsciously with a bewitching charm. Then calmly, he ate his food, remembering not to go hungry or angry into battle. Sussie was charming, but that was not all he cared for. Every now and again he answered her with grunts, aahs and oohs. Soon, she realized and she changed the subject.

How was life in England? Fine he said. And the girls? Not hot like you. Is that why you didn't marry a white girl? Possibly. I was thinking of those I left at home and their vivacity. And I had this hope that I'll be accepted, God willing. You know you are always accepted. I have not lost your place in my heart. Every year you were gone, I thought I'd never live through it. Say did you attend many dances? Oh, the balls were alright. But something African was lacking. You always had this feeling that they had plastic emotion. I mean the Music, and even the artificial dances. I couldn't cherish them after that. Gosh! That must have been boring. Let's start your rehabilitation programme at the Simba Saloon this evening. Why Not? He said, vaguely vowing to find out what it meant before they met that evening.

He was glad to get rid of her. At exactly 2 pm, he was at the office of the inspectorate chief, only to find not even the secretary. After twenty Minutes the Secretary sauntered in throwing her dangerously pleated buttocks this way and that. This annoyed him, but before he could burst, he remembered there was virtue in keeping quiet. Then he calmly asked to see the Chief Inspector. He was promptly told to wait, that the latter was having a business lunch and would be back in a moment.

****

Mr. Wambua Kauma a man of great diligence and vim was the country's top cop. Of late, motor vehicle thefts had become a fad, and were denting his image of a cops cop. There was an average of two car theft per day while a year ago, it had been two per week. Even the rate of their recovery was dismal; out of the 555 cars stolen so far, only 55 had been recovered, mostly abandoned after some robbery or an orgy or debauchery by some young pranksters. The rest it seems had melted in the tropical heat.

So, yesterday morning, before going to work, he turned on the local station, a habit he had taken on sometime in the past 47 years of his life. It seemed the President was complaining about the insecurity of the small man's property, especially their cars. He said that something had to be done about it even if it meant sacrificing a few heads. Commissioner

Wambua knew that his head must be in one of the chopping boards, ready for the man's huge political appetite.

In the morning through a signal, he called on all the patrolmen and traffic police to be extra vigilant. He also called in a special detachment of plain clothes policemen. He said that of late, discipline had broken down in his department to the extent that officers lounged lazily in the streets of Nairobi, mixing with and knowingly winking at thieves and robbers. He went on that he knew of a racket involving his service commanders who did not properly chase thieves when there was a tip off. Then he announced that he was sending them for a two month compulsory leave which must be taken out of the city, giving four hours for them to clear out of the city. With much flair, he appointed acting section commanders, increased the number of guns on the street and gave a shoot on sight order against car buglers and thieves. Then he sent the shaken, frightened and edgy policemen and women on the streets of Nairobi.

At exactly 8.30pm, Commissioner Wambua Kauma had called a press conference at traffic police headquarters, attended by heads of criminal investigations department, special branch, as well as other section heads including the crack riot police.

He announced to a hushed press corps the discovery and smashing of a car racket ring involving some of his most trusted officer's .Pressed further, he said the officers concerned were already on forced leave and that patrol had been beefed up and policemen given a shoot –ask questions later orders for suspected car thieves. Then followed more threatening speeches by the other policemen present .The head of the Special Branch declared that he had put a special tag on the head of the gang of 'Baghdad Thieves', a vicious band led by a notorious thug with the alias of Bush –El-Saddam.

Perhaps the most dramatic of all was the announcement of the C.I.D Director. He rose at stiff military attention and with precise gestures declared that the pruning of the rotten branches of society had begun that morning, and he had some warning for 'National Consumption'. With a sharp gesture, he commanded a door open and two bloody and bloodied street urchins (for that is what they looked like, and I stand to be corrected to date) were hurled into the conference room. Then with a knife edge stare, he said that those living below the accepted legal standards now knew what fate awaited them.

This stirred the press who took pictures and rushed to file the sensational story, and most forgot to ask the obvious question: what crime did these street urchins do that those who have escaped with billions of pounds of tax payers money not done? Why the urchins and scamps and not the real gangsters been caught? But probably they knew better. Their fates would have been less flattering.

Somewhere along the line, The KBC Television station, which broadcasted at scheduled hours- to save electricity, was activated unexpectedly, and through a radio announcement, those at home instantly knew that the television was transmitting. At the above spectacle, an image of criminal band of ogres marauding the city was aroused and immediately maids and housewives locked their doors.

That day, the death of the opposition leader on the precincts of parliament failed to excite the KBC Newsmen and consequently Kenyans learnt it in the Newspapers the next day when National burial arrangements were well underway. That was yesterday.

****

Today, John Nalubowe was getting mad. No public servant had permission to be out of his station of work for a long period. It was completely unacceptable. He has been kept waiting for an hour. As he prepared to ask the secretary, the door burst open and a well fed man strode in passed him and entered the office marked 'Private'. He had a tooth pick as if it was a status symbol. And without wasting time, John entered and confronted the man. The man sat with a surprised groan. He was evidently pleased with himself showing this by way of offering his business card with a list of all his decorations and occupation. DR. Eng. MBS. Holy shit, thought John.

The Chief Inspector, Nairobi City Council Inspectorate Department looked baffled, and declared to John that he knew not of him or his firm. This was pure lies. He had attended some two functions, with this same man. Couldn't this man realize?

Then John Started.

'The company I represent has a lot of business activity and interest in the country. Currently we are developing a 200 hundred acre plot in Nairobi, the subject of an injunction from your department. Please could you explain to us why you have now decided that the land after all was intended for public amenities?'

'Are you demanding me or requesting?

'I am just asking to be enlightened on new developments in our city'

'Then it will cost you to rub my back with, say, 100 thou?'

'Is that all?'

'No' the man sighed. 'The mayor knows this, I'll write to you a note to him, and then his charges would not be too much. We can't pull it off without his participation'.

In a moment, John Nalubowe had written and signed the cheque for Kenya Shillings One Hundred Thousand *only* that he exchanged that for a note to see the mayor.

The man just gave him one look and said: 'The cheque'.

John sat in front of him and wrote 200,000 shillings and gave it to His Worship. Then the mayor produced a letter rescinding the earlier decision of the Council. It was signed by both him and the Chief Inspector. As he went out, the Mayor stopped him.

'A moment, Mr Nalubowe'

'Yes' he answered, suppressing his welling anger and frustration.

'You are a dead man if the cheque bounces.' And he continued seriously perusing the documents before him. John shut the door and went out. Absent minded he went out of city hall and walked to where he had parked his car. He was reading the letter which had restored on them the authority to go ahead with the housing scheme.

Maybe it was in confusion or happiness that he found himself opening his car door. Suddenly the alarm went and as he fumbled in his pocket for the keys and the alarm button, a shot ripped through the air and rent his chest, then another and another and another. The second shot went through the hip, lodging in the hip bone, opening a vent of youthful blood; another went through his neck, ripping away his windpipe, which made enormous gurgling noises like a snoring giant.

The last shot was really unnecessary. It shattered his skull and spilled out his brains.

Immediately, the police sent a report of the shooting of a notorious car thief while resisting arrest.

The body was moved to city mortuary. His family was notified of his accidental death and the next day, the national radio announced his sudden death due to massive shock at the shooting of a goon where he was. They regretted the additional damage and clamped on any news of the ongoing police crackdown.

At the rendezvous, Sussie waited and waited in vain. Finally she went to the Simba Saloon and searched some more. She rang John's home and nobody picked the phone.

Next day, she fainted when she heard of his death. She wondered how she wouldcope with the Pay-As-You –Eat now that her most lucrative source was gone. And the Company sent its deepest condolences.

MEN OF GOD CAPITALISED

When the Most Reverend Job Kigani (B.D., D.D.-Honorary, E.B.S., and Esquire) finally retired from the Arch-Bishopric office and the seat of the metropolitan see which was the preserve of the head of our church, we all breathed a well-deserved sigh of relief. For Rev. Kigani's 'election' as Archbishop was never legitimate in our minds and, as happens with leaders of such background, his reign saw the church lurch from controversy only to limp into another.

When the archbishopric seat fell vacant, there were two clergy who were expected by the Christians to contest the seat. Only one week to the close of nomination, a consensus had been arrived at in the church leadership that there was no need to contest. It would seem that after a soul searching, one of the bishops had stepped aside for the other. This triggered subterranean chain of events that 'worked to Rev. Kigani's favour'. The archbishop-in-waiting still had a hurdle to pass. He had to become the sole nominee for the post before he could be declared 'Archbishop Elect'. The church waited with bated breath. Then it was a day to the nominations.

Searching for the papers to put in order, Bishop James Maloba of the North-West See had been startled to find them missing. His birth certificate, signed nomination forms and all the supporting documents had grown legs. A quick witted man, he had called the church chancellor who advised him to get others by 6 pm the next day. He promptly got others and started the process all over. Needless to say, at 5.30 p.m. the next day, he was still searching for the Right Reverend Job Kigani, who was to be his second recommender. It looked as if there was going to be no nomination for the archbishop's seat and the chancellor was beginning to arrange for his departure when the Right Reverend Job Kigani calmly walked in. The lawyer looked surprised and pleased at the same time. A man whose ear was on the ground, he knew that Rev. Kigani must have come to do only one thing: hand in nomination papers on behalf of Bishop Maloba.

He accepted the papers with his usual 'jolly good' utterance, and congratulated himself for trusting in God. As he perused them more

105

closely, he indulged in a strangled cry of unbelief and his jaw sagged. He uttered only one word: 'disaster' and started initialling the nomination papers which, after all, were in order.

'Well, chancellor, how many are contesting for the archbishops seat?'
'There's no contest', he managed in a strangled voice.
'I would have thought, would one not, that this seat would excite a lot of interest. But it seems God's will that its responsibilities fall on my under serving shoulders' Rev. Kigani persisted.
'Yes, yes. God's will.'
'I hope to work with you fruitfully'.
'No need to hope, Bwana Archbishop Elect. I prepared a resignation letter just in case – effective from the date of your enthronement'.
'In that case, I wish you well in your endeavours,' the Right Reverend, future Most Reverend Kigani informed the outgoing chancellor, banally, though with studied contempt.
'I am calling the press for a briefing. Want a word with them?'
'No need for you to arrange for me one. Thanks all the same'.
'I have a formal celebration. Care to join us?'
'Thanks for the gesture, but I am indisposed – stomach upsets. I am getting old, you know.'
'I understand', the Archbishop elect intoned in that peculiarly priestly voice he had.

So that evening, the Right Reverend James Maloba was at home watching television. He was also waiting for the chancellor to ring him with the news that the nominations had been postponed to a later date when an item in the news caught his attention. With shock, he learnt that the bishop he had been waiting for to sign his nomination papers had become the sole nominee for the archbishopric, and therefore the Archbishop elect. With two other bishops who were themselves facing disciplinary matters with the church tribunal which he (Rev.Maloba) chaired, Kigani was celebrating and announcing the programme to guide the church up to the year 2000 and beyond.

So for twenty years (it is significant that his reign did not take us to the year 2000), The Most Reverend, His Grace, Dr Job Kigani, B.D., D.D., (Hon.), E.B.S., Esquire presided over a church in wilderness. Unlike Moses, he had the disadvantage of not being chosen of God, and even when he preached the most inspired sermon, his congregation had the habit of seeing a question mark sitting over and above the Mitre.

So the retirement of this man of God on 29 August, 1996 was no mean achievement. The Christians felt like giving him a medal of courage, like the one the British gave to its citizens who helped in the colonial service. Something like the D.S.O. would have come in handy.

But if the church was going to find it difficult choosing an archbishop, this was the time. For his Grace's retirement left the church like a lamb amid a pack of wolves. One of the questions of the church was: Do we give to Ceaser what is his? And if so, who should be the Ceaser? And if the church gave to Ceaser, did it on behalf of its member Christians have the moral duty to ask Ceaser to account for the Dinars so given?

As in argument, there was bound to be two sides, and the neutral camp that in its dubiety sought to eat their cake and yet have it.

On one issue, there was amorphous consensus – both sides agreed that Ceaser was here and his purse needed filling. There, the consensus stopped. One group insisted there was no need to ask Ceaser for the bills of expenditure, and that to do this would prove that one aspires for Ceasarship. The palace of Caesar was not the church. They advised anyone asking Caesar for accountability to jump from the boat of Christ and into the ship of state. They further claimed that the church had to shun what comes out of the dirty purse of Caesar. As we later learnt, these men of God were actually eating out of Caesars purse. This group was represented in the race for the archbishop seat by the Rev. Johannes Mulindwa.

The other camp consisted of the 'diehard'. They insisted that although they gave money to Caesar on the basis of trust, they had a responsibility to see that Christians received the service so promised. To this end, they insisted that Christians should discard the mundane notion that this world was not their home and participate fully in its affairs. They sought as a first step to educate the Christians on the need to vote, and the type of choices that will render good service.

This group no doubt elicited the wrath of Caesar. The public radio and television started a snipping campaign against two of the leading clergy in this group. The clerics, it was said, were known to preach water and drink wine. This phrase was said too repeatedly that we began to believe it was the case. The clerics campaign against Caesar dampened somehow as they were forced to answer some very specific allegations which were beginning to hurt their reputations. However, two weeks to nominations, the Right Reverend Paul Apollo withdrew from the race declaring that his perceived 'extremism' would not help in building and uniting the church. Now, only Rev. Milungo remained from the 'radical camp'.

A soft spoken man, Rev. Milungo was not just a trained pastor, but also a born one. His ability to listen and feel compassion was almost infinite. He was a Bishop with a 'testimony' as well as 'the gospel'. This blend of qualities was proving so formidable that Rev. Johannes Mulindwa began looking like the loser he was. Rev. Milungo did not seem to campaign. He did not talk about the election and went on ministering to God's people. His preaching engagements were numerous. He seemed able to find time to counsel all those with problems, he was never behind schedule in his ecclesiastical duties.

When the house of bishops met one week to the election, he was given time and preached for over an hour on Christian reproachment and reconciliation. They therefore agreed to put aside personal differences and appear together in front of Christians. All bishops and senior clergy were urged to attend the closing of our annual convention. This happened to be the eve of nomination.

As a staunch Christian, I could never miss a convention. For it is in the convention where the flagging spirit is strengthened. It is an event attended by Christians of all convictions. Take as example the many fellowship groups in our church. There is this fellowship group that is distinct because they do not allow their women to grow long hair. They also forbid them wearing any items of beauty of whatever nature. They derive their strength from Paul's letter to the Corinthians and stress the verse that compels a woman to submit to men, so that men may submit to Jesus on their behalf. They insist that in any case, a woman must always cover her hair.

There is this other group which insist that Christians must not eat a wedding cake. They insist that a wedding cake originated from pagan practices in the Middle East in the period immediately after the death of Christ. Wasn't it the type of feasting that Paul cautioned the Corinthians about?

The third group, no less holy, sang as their anthem 'this world is not my home'. They shunned everything worldly and said that their granaries were full in heaven. They believed they could do no wrong so long as they shunned the company of the worldly. They lay a strong emphasis on 'give unto Caesar what is his and to God what is God's'. Moreover, they insisted that Christians must wash their dirty linen in public. Nevertheless, once a year, they would shed their reclusiveness and attend the great convention of our church.

There was yet another group that was distinguished by their predilection towards 'speaking in tongues'. This group insisted that they were spirit filled, and one who was spirit filled always spoke in tongues. This group was the most exclusive since many of us were unable to speak in tongues. I often asked them what it profited God to speak in a tongue strange to his people. They would then wave me away haughtily.

These were not the only groups. There was those that believed that 'faith without works was dead', and that 'the kingdom of God was like the fourteen maids', and other of equally mundane if weird leanings.

I will just describe for you the order of events in our conventions. On the last day, the convention is opened by the numerous choirs that set the mood for the evening. When the choirs are done with, choruses follow only to be replaced by a session of individual prayers interspersed with tongue speaking. The Christians' blossom into flowers of the spirit' as one believer once described it. A hymn followed by dedication prayer ushers in preacher. The Rt. Rev. Mulindwa prayed to God to guide the preacher' to deliver only what is truly of your mouth, and so that your spirit may be made manifest among men'. He omitted that it may also dwell among women. You will please include me among the group that felt that the man of God needed to be touched by the spirit himself. It is one of the mysteries of God's ways that you may pray to others and they get touched yet you yourself remain unblessed. You don't expect he sat down without making a dig at Rev. Milungo.

'Lord, we note that the church is teetering on the brink of the edge of your kingdom towards darkness. You demand of us absolute service, and to fix our faces on your righteous home in heaven. But Lord there are those among us even now that will compete Caesar for this world. Let them who would they governed the world, and were counted among the goats when the son of man come, to throw down their collars and go into the world. But as for me blessed lord, I pick up my cross and follow you!'

He emphatically finished with what looked like a triumphant gleam radiating from his face. Was it the gleam of victory over sin? Or was the race for the archbishop's seat already won? But I did not have time to ponder the imponderables as the Rev. Milungo's baritone came over the speakers.
'...though your sins may be scarlet, I will wipe them away and you will be as white as snow. Come now, let us reason together, the Lord says'. These words are the words of wisdom that the Lord imparts on us tonight.
'For many of us, the imagery of scarlet and snow may not strike us with forceful dichotomy. We need to vary the reporting of the Holy Bible. For us the ultimate expression of the colour red is blood – not scarlet. When it flows, it means only one thing: murder, mayhem, destruction; evil. These are the epithets the word scarlet combines. Then of course we have the snow. Most of us have never seen snow because we don't live near the mountain – top, or in the cold lands. But we have seen hailstones, and they are as white as snow. Yet others will only have seen the cattle egrets, and

110

in them we see the ultimate expression of innocence, purity and harmony; good. We see life expressed and respected.

The prophet of God used these two extremes of reflect the gulf that through man's fault developed between human beings and God. It is a gulf which no human exertion could hope to bridge. It is a gulf that is detrimental as it is debilitating to man. And that is why with humility he says, 'Come now, let us reason together'.

'In the two verses we have quoted, God offers us two things through his grace. He says that just by lifting your voice in confession and allowing righteousness to reign in your heart, He like a painter will rub off the stain of vermillion with a stroke of his white brush of mercy. And his Mercy is such that all your past will be forgotten – like a garment which burns to ashes. It will become dazzling white and you will receive a new baptism – and your new name will be written in the book of life. You will be created, begin to exist, gain form and join the list of Gods children. But to continue staying in your folly, to refuse to confess, to join the train of life will lead only to perdition, oblivion and death'.

'But how God loves us sinners though we are! He knows we are errant not because we will but because our heads are stuffed with worldly doubts. We pout and are peevish like little children when we cannot understand his ways. Unlike Job, we cannot understand why he gives and takes away. We become despondent when we don't eat bread in the morning despite praying for it. We are chagrined when our loved one die and God seems not to care. When we lose our jobs, love, wealth, prestige…. We begin to check our CV's in the service of his church and ask why it is, why it is, that God keeps aloof while his people suffer? And those who have not confessed also ask: if God loves us so, why can't Hehelp the saved in our midst?'

'Christian, the kingdom of God was only won by the bloodshed at Calvary. I tell you truly, you have not sacrificed even one bit as our Lord did! He left his throne and became small in our midst. He suffered abuses, beatings and was himself tortured and murdered for the sake of the kingdom. What have you given!?

'And because of your folly, because of your small mindedness, your impertinence, your incapacity to comprehend his infinite wisdom, He's willing to sit down again with you to reason!'
'Think of it, just the two of you, you and God heart to heart. He will demean himself a second time for your sake – to talk to you! What trouble God goes through for our salvation shows just how important our lives are. Are you willing to go an extra mile for a rendezvous with God? I call upon you whose tongues have been heavy until now to come and confess!'

He finished emphatically and the atmosphere was charged with the electricity that fills the air in the aftermath of lighting. The congregation burst into the Christian anthem 'Amazing Grace'. Many souls came to be saved. One man even produced a bag of over Kshs. 2,000 he had stolen during 'Sadaka'. An adulterous man who had come in search of a woman during the convention and had been canoodling with her owned up but was stopped short before he could name the woman in question.

A politician promised to return the plot he had grabbed from the land meant for the expansion of our National Hospital. A church treasurer confessed that she had been creaming off collections from the church. A government chief revealed that he had been imposing and collecting illegal tax in the name of 'Harambee'. A school teacher confessed how she…but the confessions were becoming hairier, weirder by the minute.

Then one woman of striking beauty stood up. In a sopranoic voice full of trilling cadence, she declared that she wanted to rededicate her life to God. She asked the preacher to join her and Rev. Milungo, in Christian charity and usual sympathy went and attempted to pray with her by placing his hands on her head. This apparently gave the woman the spur she had been waiting for. Madly shouting at Rev. Milungo, she railed: 'Hypocrite! Adulterer! How many times have you tasted the sweetness of my Loins! Yes, you liar! You preach to us the message that should apply to you! I have given birth to three children, all yours. Are you not ashamed of conning other Christians with your message? Oh may a righteous priest come and lay hands on me for my forgiveness!'

(I must say if it were an ordinary sinner like me, it would not gall me for such a woman to broadcast my indiscretions with her). Like a dog released from its leash, Rev Mulindwa sprang into action. Rev. Milungo was thunderstruck. He could not move. He tried to invoke the spirit that spoke through the woman. But the Right Reverend Mulindwa shooed him away and started offering prayers for 'our sister Rose'. The name became popular immediately.

The convention ended in total bedlam if not chaos. There broke fistfights between the supporters of Rev. Mulindwa who were openly jeering at the fall of Rev. Milungo, and the latter's zealots. By now it became clear that the Rev. Milungo could not hope to marshal untainted respect from the whole church, even if he won the seat of archbishop.
To waiting newspaper men, Rev. Milungo declared that he was withdrawing his candidature for the seat.

'Does that mean that the allegations by these women are true?'
'It doesn't have to be a confirmation or denial, seeing as it is that only time can look upon such claims favourably and exonerate if not vindicate me.'
'Reverend, why are you being cagey about your unmasking?' asked yet another pushy reporter.
'May God forgive that woman for what she had done.' Answered Rev. Milungo.
'Do you intend to sue her for libel?'
'To what purpose? That woman deserves sympathy, not litigation.'
'One more question er...Reverend. Who will you support for the archbishops seats? Will you support Rev. Mulindwa?"
'Who will God support? Obviously the best pastor to preside over his church. It does not matter who I support.'
'Are we to understand that Rev. Mulindwa becomes the new Archbishop?'
'If God wills.' Answered Rev. Milungo as he entered his car.

The next day, we went to wait at the National Cathedral where the nomination papers would be received. We were praying inwardly that an opponent comes forward to vie with Rev. Mulindwa. We viewed his possible ascension to the seat and heart of our church with a feeling of doom. But at times doom looks so inevitable. Monday 2, October 1996, 5 pm we were still waiting. No Bishop had appeared. The present church chancellor waited with a thin smile as he contemplated the moment when Rev. Mulindwa would make a theatrical entry to stake his claim. He was familiar with the backroom politics that had made Job Kigani become archbishop and that has now broken the back of Rev. Milungo. The church, he knew, was a long way from gaining a voice. Rev. Mulindwa was unstable – unfit for any ecclesiastical post. But he was the available material and Ceaser knew you could only use the available material.

5.55 PM. He did not like it one bit. Rev. Mulindwa was extending theatrics too far. Then a person with a radio among the crowd gathered outside the church burst out into a loud AMEN!

In a jiffy, the news of Rev. Mulindwa's death had travelled far. In the seven O'clock evening news, it was reported that the car he was travelling in with 'our sister Rose' had plunged into a ravine. Their bodies' shew evidence of carousal.
Nobody knew where they were from or to.
It had become clear that we were yet to have an archbishop. We are still waiting with bated breath.

www.ingramcontent.com/pod-product-compliance
Lightning Source LLC
Chambersburg PA
CBHW060644130626
46555CB00002B/955